DAILY GRAMS: GUIDED REVIEW AIDING MASTERY SKILLS

Author: Wanda C. Phillips

Published by ISHA Enterprises, Inc.
Easy Grammar Systems
Post Office Box 12520
Scottsdale, Arizona   85267
Website: www.easygrammar.com
© 1987

ISBN   0-936981-05-9

DEDICATION

DAILY GRAMS: Guided Review Aiding Mastery Skills is dedicated with love to our children's wonderful "GRAMS," Frances Marie Kuykendall and Thelma Lee Phillips Goff.

The purpose of **DAILY GRAMS: GUIDED REVIEW AIDING MASTERY SKILLS** is to provide students with **daily** review of their language. Bringing this information to the "forefront" of one's memory will help to insure **mastery learning**.

FORMAT

You will note that each page is set up in this manner:

1. Sentence one will always contain **capitalization** errors. Encourage students to write only the words that should be capitalized.

2. In sentence 2 of each exercise, students will insert needed **punctuation**. It is suggested that students write out this sentence, adding proper punctuation.

3. Both sentences 3 and 4 will be **general review**. You may want to replace one of these items with material you are currently studying.

4. Sentence 5 is always a **sentence combining**. Using sentences given, students will write one, more intricate sentence. This helps the student move to higher levels of writing. If you feel that the sentences given are too difficult for your level, simply delete parts. In most cases, you have been given two possible answers. Needless to say, there are more.

DAILY GRAMS: GUIDED REVIEW AIDING MASTERY SKILLS is designed as a guided review. There are 180 "GRAMS" in this book, one review per teaching day. **DAILY GRAMS** will take approximately **10 minutes** total time; this includes both doing and grading.

PROCEDURE:

1. Students should be **trained** to do "GRAMS" immediately upon entering the classroom. Therefore, "GRAMS" should be copied, written on the chalkboard, or placed on a transparency for use with an overhead projector. (The items on each page have been placed closely so that the entire lesson will fit onto an overhead projector. Of course, the projector will need to be adjusted to enlarge the print.)

2. Students will finish at different rates. Two ideas are suggested:

    A. Require students to have a reading book with them **at all times**. Students simply read when finished.

    B. Allow students "Three Minute Conversations" when they have completed **DAILY GRAMS**. Students will select a partner and discuss anything (within limits of school suitability). The requirement is that all thoughts are expressed in **complete** sentences. Those who work faster may get the entire three minutes while others may only get a minute or two. The purpose, however, is that everyone is ready to check "GRAMS" at the same time.

3. Go over the answers as a class orally. In making students accountable for this type of activity, you may wish to take a quiz grade occasionally.

SUGGESTIONS

1. It is suggested that "GRAMS" be transferred to transparencies, numbered, and filed. In using them over a period of years, one only has to draw the "GRAMS" from the file.

2. The blackboard may also be used.

3. Some teachers will want to make copies for each student. In doing this, a master copy for students or the teacher to give answers is advisable.

4. Solicit as much student response as possible.

5. As one progresses through this book, some of the sentences become longer and more complex. This may necessitate an adaptation to your own teaching needs.

STUDENT RESPONSE TO **DAILY GRAMS**

"GRAMS helps me to get my mind going when I get to English class."

"I think GRAMS helps me to remember everything we learned."

"They help me remember things I forgot."

"I'm learning a lot about sentence combining."

"I really like the GRAMS. I think they are fun, and we can learn from them."

"I really enjoy GRAMS. I think that they keep the material I have learned in my head."

CAPITALIZATION:

1. my mom went to school at mesa high school.

PUNCTUATION:

2. The answer in fact is in the book

PARTS OF SPEECH:

3. What part of speech is **honesty**?

PARTS OF SPEECH: Verbs

       Determine the correct past participle; underline the verb phrase:

4. The cat has _____ (drank, drunk) all of its milk.

SENTENCE COMBINING:

5. The boy threw an eraser.
   The boy was angry.
   The boy threw the eraser at his sister.

Day 2

CAPITALIZATION:

1. last summer our family went to yellowstone national park.

PUNCTUATION:

2. Mary have you seen my binoculars

PARTS OF SPEECH: Adjectives
      Select adjectives.

3. The beautiful white swan swam on a peaceful pond.

PARTS OF SPEECH: Nouns
      Write the **plural** of the nouns:

4. A. child
   B. moose
   C. ox

SENTENCE COMBINING:

5. The child was lost.
   The child was crying.
   The child was looking for her mother.

CAPITALIZATION:

1. we saw judge barnworth at a kiwanis club meeting.

PUNCTUATION:

2. Jill exclaimed Give me the ticket

DIRECT OBJECTS:

 Select the direct object.

3. After dinner, we put the milk in the refrigerator.

PARTS OF SPEECH: Nouns

4. What kind of noun is **peace**?

SENTENCE COMBINING:

5. The show would soon begin.
 The show was a puppet show.
 Everyone crowded quickly into the auditorium.

Day 4

CAPITALIZATION:

1. did napoleon lose at the battle of waterloo?

PUNCTUATION:

2. The correct route to take I believe is Route 42

SENTENCE TYPES:

> Determine the sentence type (declarative, imperative, interrogative, or exclamatory).

3. A. Go to the front of the room.
    B. Your pencil is on the floor.

PARTS OF SPEECH: Verbs

4. **To + verb** is called an _____.

SENTENCE COMBINING:

5. The horse roamed over the countryside.
    The horse was black.
    The horse was homeless.

CAPITALIZATION:

1. the title of the book is <u>success through a positive mental attitude</u>.

PUNCTUATION:

2. That address should be 500 Willow Lane Atlanta Georgia

PARTS OF SPEECH: Nouns

3. In forming plural nouns, words ending with _____, _____, _____, _____, and _____ add **es**.

PARTS OF SPEECH: Adverbs

Select the adverbs that tell **when** in the sentence.

4. Study now, but take the test later.

SENTENCE COMBINING:

5. A ring was lost.
The ring was an emerald and diamond one.
The ring was valued at ten thousand dollars.

Day 6

CAPITALIZATION:

1. the red cross association met last friday with governor jonas t. phelps.

PUNCTUATION:

2. I want a milkshake said Tony

DIRECT OBJECTS:

>   Determine the direct object.

3. The runner finished that race in ten minutes.

SUBJECTS/VERBS:

>   Underline the subject once and the verb/verb phrase twice.

4. Have the car owner and the insurance company agreed to a settlement?

SENTENCE COMBINING:

5. The car was stalled.
    The car was in the middle of the intersection.
    It was raining.

CAPITALIZATION:

1. should I have asked grandma to meet us at rustlers' restaurant?

PUNCTUATION:

2. My family and I went to Bangor Maine last summer

PARTS OF SPEECH: Verbs

       Choose the past participle; underline the verb phrase.

3. That candidate has _____ (ran, run) in nearly every election.

SUBJECTS/VERBS:

       Underline the subject once and the verb/verb phrase twice.

4. Either Tom or his brother will be going on the skiing trip.

SENTENCE COMBINING:

5. Lori's mother is in the church choir.
    Lori's mother sang a solo.
    Lori's mother sang her solo last Sunday.

CAPITALIZATION:

1. washington, d.c., is located in the east.

PUNCTUATION:

2. Because school wasnt open John went to the mall

SUBJECTS/VERBS:

Underline the subject once and the verb/verb phrase twice.

3. Give the message to Harold, please.

SENTENCE TYPES:

Determine the sentence type (declarative, interrogative, imperative, or exclamatory).

4. A. Are the tulips blooming?
   B. This is ridiculous!

SENTENCE COMBINING:

5. Dr. Marlowe is a veterinarian.
   Dr. Marlowe has given our dog a shot.
   Our dog's leg was infected.

CAPITALIZATION:

1. the papago indian reservation is located in eastern arizona.

PUNCTUATION:

2. Harrys birthday is Feb 28 1987

PARTS OF SPEECH: Verbs

　　　Determine if the verb is action or linking.

3. A. Has Lou ever tasted artichokes?
　 B. This milk tastes sour.

PARTS OF SPEECH: Nouns

4. What type of noun is **air**?

SENTENCE COMBINING:

5. The children played in the sand.
　 The children were laughing.
　 The children made sand castles.

Day 10

CAPITALIZATION:

1. an alaskan cruise is scheduled to leave for the aleutian islands.

PUNCTUATION:

2. On Saturday March 7 1927 they were married

PARTS OF SPEECH: Verbs
       Determine if the verb is action or linking.

3. A. We <u>felt</u> our way along the darkened passage.

   B. A student <u>felt</u> sick after lunch.

PARTS OF SPEECH: Nouns
       Write the plural of the nouns.

4. A. bug
   B. mouse
   C. deer
   D. watch

SENTENCE COMBINING:

5. The policewoman stopped the driver.
The driver had been speeding.
The driver was given a ticket.

CAPITALIZATION:

1. has fanny's fudge factory moved downtown to brookside drive?

PUNCTUATION:

2. Tom Sweeny the store manager will give you a refund Susan

SUBJECTS/VERBS:

     Determine subject and verb.

3. One of the students left his book and returned for it.

PARTS OF SPEECH: Adjectives

     Determine adjectives in the sentence.

4. Ominous black clouds darkened the bright sky.

SENTENCE COMBINING:

5. Jill is an only child.
   Jill is spoiled.
   Jill is allowed to do what she wishes.

Day 12

CAPITALIZATION:

1. my aunt tara bought carmichael* ice cream at romero's drugstore.
brand name

PUNCTUATION:

2. Although Kami wont visit shell send cards

PARTS OF SPEECH: Adjectives
      Determine the predicate adjective.

3. Your sleek black coat is very warm.

PARTS OF SPEECH: Verbs

4. Write six auxiliary (helping) verbs.

SENTENCE COMBINING:

5. The vase was broken.
    The vase lay in small pieces on the floor.
    The vase was an antique.

CAPITALIZATION:

1. have you visited the kansas state fair each fall, wendy?

PUNCTUATION:

2. Your reading test will be tomorrow be sure to study

PARTS OF SPEECH: Verbs

      Select the past participle form; then underline the verb phrase.

3. The vehicle had been _____(stole, stolen).

PARTS OF SPEECH: Pronouns

      Determine the correct pronoun.

4. James and _____(I, me) want to go.

SENTENCE COMBINING:

5. The milk is sour.
   Tom left the milk out.
   The milk is chocolate.

Day 14

CAPITALIZATION:

1. in reading, our class enjoyed the book, <u>the tales of two cities</u>.

PUNCTUATION:

2. No youre not to blame it isnt anyones fault

PARTS OF SPEECH: Prepositions

Cross out any prepositional phrases.

3. During the storm several trees fell by the side of the road.

PARTS OF SPEECH: Nouns

Write a proper noun for each common one.

4. A. river
   B. person
   C. bank
   D. school

SENTENCE COMBINING:

5. The restaurant served breakfast.
   Jill didn't want to go there.
   Jill wanted to eat at a cafeteria.

CAPITALIZATION:

1. the french poodle was taken to uptown grooming shoppe last saturday.

PUNCTUATION:

2. Joes dad a lawyer flew to Omaha Nebraska today

PARTS OF SPEECH: Nouns
        Determine nouns.

3. Her hair had been cut in a nice salon.

PARTS OF SPEECH: Verbs

4. Write six helping verbs.

SENTENCE COMBINING:

5. The chef cut the vegetables.
   The chef fried the fish.
   The chef was Oriental.
   The chef cooked at our table.

Day 16

CAPITALIZATION:

1. do mr. and mrs. colena attend a baptist church in iowa?

PUNCTUATION:

2. We purchased French fries a shake and a hamburger Vince

CONJUNCTIONS:

3. Write the three most commonly used coordinating conjunctions.

SUBJECTS/VERBS:

Underline the subject once and the verb/verb phrase twice.

4. John's sister changed jobs and now works part-time.

SENTENCE COMBINING:

5. The clock was broken.
    The clock was a digital one.
    The clock had been given to my father as a gift.

CAPITALIZATION:

1. has my uncle purchased german potato salad at the deli?

PUNCTUATION:

2. Do you Marsha have a sketch for the childrens playground

PHRASES/CLAUSES:

A clause has subject and verb; a phrase is a group of words.

3. **Phrase** or **Clause**?   Jane went to the zoo.

PARTS OF SPEECH:

4. What part of speech is **"OH!"** ?

SENTENCE COMBINING:

5. The potted tulip was a gift.
   The tulip is dying.
   Grandma gave it to Mom.

Day 18

CAPITALIZATION:

1. was century elementary school closed for valentine's day?

PUNCTUATION:

2. I Birds
      A Types
         1 Migrating
         2 Non-migrating
      B Habitats

PARTS OF SPEECH: Adverbs

    Select any adverbs that tell **when**.

3. Yesterday, we should have gone sooner.

PARTS OF SPEECH: Verbs

    Select the correct past participle; underline the verb phrase.

4. I shouldn't have _____(drank, drunk) so much water.

SENTENCE COMBINING:

5. Flowers had been planted in the garden.
   Jim had planted them.
   Jim had forgotten to water them.

CAPITALIZATION:

1. last spring we read about a swiss village in geography class.

PUNCTUATION:

2. This rug most certainly was made in China

PARTS OF SPEECH: Verbs
     Select the verb that agrees with the subject.

3. The duck (swim, swims) slowly.

SUBJECTS/VERBS:
     Underline the subject once; underline the verb/verb phrase twice.

4. Letters, bills, and stamps were lying on the table.

SENTENCE COMBINING:

5. The book was about wildlife.
The book was on the table.
The book was open to a chapter about moose.

Day 20

CAPITALIZATION:

1. each year the smith family goes to the pasadena tournament of roses parade in california.

PUNCTUATION:

2. Did Mary the junior cheerleader go with you

PHRASES/CLAUSES:

Remember: A clause has a subject and a verb.

3. Even though the rain slackened.

PARTS OF SPEECH: Verbs

Select the verb that agrees with the subject.

4. The nurses (works, work) on holidays.

SENTENCE COMBINING:

5. Lunch was served at noon.
Soup and sandwiches were served.
They were delicious.

CAPITALIZATION:

1. some dutch tulips were growing by metrocenter mall in phoenix.

PUNCTUATION:

2. What she asked is the answer to the problem

PARTS OF SPEECH: Nouns
       Determine the direct object, if any.

3. Bill threw the paper at me.

SUBJECTS/VERBS:

4. One of the children (was, were) playing in the water.

SENTENCE COMBINING:

5. The typewriter was repaired.
   The typewriter was repaired by Mr. Samuels.
   The repairing cost $9.00.

Day 22

CAPITALIZATION:

1. at christmas, we flew into kennedy airport in new york.

PUNCTUATION:

2. No your answer to say the least wasnt wrong

PARTS OF SPEECH: Verbs

3. List 8 helping (auxiliary) verbs.

PARTS OF SPEECH: Nouns

   Select nouns.

4. That center for learning was opened in June.

SENTENCE COMBINING:

5. The waiter served the salad.
   The waiter dropped the fork.
   The waiter was embarrassed.

CAPITALIZATION:

1. my uncle jim drives over the potomac river to his job at the department of education.

PUNCTUATION:

2. Your ts need to be crossed but the other letters are fine

PARTS OF SPEECH: Verbs

3. Each of the children (need, needs) lunch.

SENTENCE TYPES:

   Determine the type of sentence.

4. Go away.
   A. declarative   B. interrogative   C. imperative   D. exclamatory

SENTENCE COMBINING:

5. My sister put wallpaper in the kitchen.
   The wallpaper was green and flowered.
   The wallpaper fell off the wall.

Day 24

CAPITALIZATION:

1. during easter vacation, our troop visited sell's nursing home on west palm lane.

PUNCTUATION:

2.   22 East Dow
                                                      Gettysburg PA 17325
                                                      January 21 2004

   Dear Mrs Parks

FRIENDLY LETTERS:

3. Determine the two parts of the friendly letter in #2.

PARTS OF SPEECH: Verbs
        Select the correct verb; underline the verb phrase.

4. Your friend should not have (come, came) with us.

SENTENCE COMBINING:

5. The floor is sticky.
   Honey has been spilled on it.
   The floor needs to be washed.

CAPITALIZATION:

1. are the great plains in the midwest?

PUNCTUATION:

2. Giant black ants emerged from the ground and marched across the lawn

PARTS OF SPEECH: Verbs

3. Write the future tense of **to stay**.

FRAGMENTS:

   Change the fragment to a sentence.

4. Running down the street.

SENTENCE COMBINING:

5. The yard was filled with mud.
   Joe went there to play.

Day 26

CAPITALIZATION:

1. the members of st. james lutheran church participated in a columbus day parade.

PUNCTUATION:

2. If Lieut Jones cant join us lets go to a show

PARTS OF SPEECH: Nouns
        Circle nouns.

3. A cookie jar was on the top of the refrigerator.

SUBJECTS/VERBS:
        Underline the subject once and the verb/verb phrase twice.

4. Give this to your dad.

SENTENCE COMBINING:

5. A beautician cut the client's hair.
   The client's hair was long.
   It is now a short bob.

CAPITALIZATION:

1. the <u>bible</u> is written in spanish in mexico.

PUNCTUATION:

2. I need the following eggs milk and bread

DIRECT OBJECTS:

      Determine the direct object.

3. The coach handed a ribbon to me.

INDIRECT OBJECTS:

      Determine the indirect object.

4. The coach handed the player a ribbon.

SENTENCE COMBINING:

5. Jane went skiing at Vail.
   Jane had a good time.
   Jane went with her family.

Day 28

CAPITALIZATION:

1. did you know that hiawatha was an iroquois indian who lived in the east?

PUNCTUATION:

2. The streets were flooded therefore only large trucks used it ~~it~~ them

PARTS OF SPEECH: Adjectives

Determine the comparative adjective form.

3. Our baby kitten is (more energetic, most energetic) than its mother.

PARTS OF SPEECH: Nouns

Write the plural.

4. A. monkey

B. brook

C. octopus

D. secretary

E. goose

SENTENCE COMBINING:

5. The heel of the shoe was broken.
The shoe belongs to Jeanie.
Jeanie threw the shoe away.

CAPITALIZATION:

1. we found franco's* applesauce on the shelf at begay's grocery.
*brand name

PUNCTUATION:

2. Use a three pronged fork to pitch the hay said the farmer

SUBJECTS/VERBS:

> Underline the subject once and the verb/verb phrase twice.

3. Neither the principal nor the teachers could attend the meeting.

PARTS OF SPEECH: Adverbs

> Determine any adverbs that tell **to what extent**.

4. Dad was too tired to be very angry.

SENTENCE COMBINING:

5. The dolphins performed.
The children were happy.
The children watched eagerly.

Day 30

CAPITALIZATION:

1. the museum of natural history had an exhibit of arctic artifacts.

PUNCTUATION:

2. The story entitled All Summer in a Day is in the book Thrust

SUBJECTS/VERBS:

Determine the subject and verb/verb phrase.

3. Our neighbors hadn't introduced themselves.

PARTS OF SPEECH: Pronouns

Select the correct pronoun.

4. Martha runs faster than _____ (I, me).

SENTENCE COMBINING:

5. The girls went to the library.
   The girls then went ice skating.
   The girls ice skated for two hours.

CAPITALIZATION:

1. the country of england is bordered by the atlantic ocean and the north sea.

PUNCTUATION:

2. We cleaned the house and Mom gave the car a tune up

PARTS OF SPEECH: Nouns
      Determine any nouns.

3. I want a book with strange pictures of spaceships.

FRIENDLY LETTERS:

4. Label the parts of a friendly letter.

_____
_____ A.
_____

_____ B.

_____
_____ C.
_____

_____ D.
_____ E.

SENTENCE COMBINING:

5. The weather is sunny.
   The forecast is for rain.
   A picnic is planned.

Day 32

CAPITALIZATION:

1. the ship, <u>u.s.s. constitution,</u> was pictured in our history book, <u>all about history</u>.

PUNCTUATION:

2. On Feb 14 1912 Arizona was admitted to the Union

PHRASES/CLAUSES:

3. The meeting time was changed.

PARTS OF SPEECH: Adverbs
       Select adverb(s) that tell **how**.

4. Determinedly, Betty hit the ball hard.

SENTENCE COMBINING:

5. The house was painted.
    Professional painters did the job.
    The owners were pleased.

CAPITALIZATION:

1. when brian came to oak junior college, he was assigned to dr. coe's calculus I class.

PUNCTUATION:

2. Joe retorted Are you by the way leaving Id like a ride

PARTS OF SPEECH: Pronouns

 Select the correct possessive form.

3. Everybody left _____ (his, their) books.

SUBJECTS/VERBS:

 Underline the subject once and the verb/verb phrase twice.

4. Is one of the fishermen entertaining us?

SENTENCE COMBINING:

5. The story is in our English book.
 The same story is in our reading book.
 The story is "The Cask of Amontillado."

Day 34

CAPITALIZATION:

1. the movie, <u>the last of the mohicans,</u> was playing at brack's theater.

PUNCTUATION:

2. The book Mother Gooses Tales contained the nursery rhyme entitled Hickory Dickory Dock

PARTS OF SPEECH: Verbs
Select the correct verb.

3. The carpenter (lay, laid) the tile in the kitchen.

PARTS OF SPEECH: Verbs
Write the past participle form:

4. A. to throw
   B. to swear
   C. to lie (to rest)
   D. to give
   E. to burst

SENTENCE COMBINING:

5. The tree is in bloom.
   The tree is a dogwood.
   It is spring.

CAPITALIZATION:

1. the poem, "my life has changed," begins, "i knew you once..."

PUNCTUATION:

2. Twenty one of the eighty four or one fourth was the answer

PARTS OF SPEECH: Adjectives
  Select the adjectives.

3. That new couch was stained with dirty smudges.

PARTS OF SPEECH: Verbs

4. Write the future tense of **to speak**.

SENTENCE COMBINING:

5. The pamphlets tell about Utah.
   The pamphlets are free.
   The pamphlets are to encourage tourism.

Day 36

CAPITALIZATION:

1. if you, sharon, favored staying with the american colonists during the american revolution, you knew about the boston massacre.

PUNCTUATION:

2. Ms Simms said Please come to my office

PARTS OF SPEECH: Adjectives

A predicate adjective occurs in the predicate and describes the subject.
Select the predicate adjective.

3. His rocking horse is blue.

SENTENCE TYPES:

Determine the type of sentence: interrogative, imperative, declarative, exclamatory.

4. There have been five fire drills.

SENTENCE COMBINING:

5. The painting is hanging in the living room.
The painting is crooked.
The painting is by McGrew.

CAPITALIZATION:

1. the newspaper article, "the testing of intelligence," disagrees with most experts.

PUNCTUATION:

2. Tom Sellers D D S is offering free dental check ups

PHRASES/CLAUSES:

3. Although the fish were biting.

PARTS OF SPEECH: Adverbs

Select any adverbs that tell **how**.

4. Joe runs steadily and fast.

SENTENCE COMBINING:

5. The garden was planted in May.
   Beans and carrots were planted.
   The vegetables are growing nicely.

Day 38

CAPITALIZATION:

1. during the ice age, the atlantic ocean was a mass of ice.

PUNCTUATION:

2. If you leave early lock the door Mary

PARTS OF SPEECH: Verbs

    Select the correct form; underline the verb phrase twice.

3. They have (swum, swam) on the school team before.

SUBJECTS/VERBS:

    Underline the subject once and the verb/verb phrase twice.

4. Some of the wild geese had flown south for the winter.

SENTENCE COMBINING:

5. The purse was lying on the ground.
   The contents were scattered on the sidewalk.
   Theo helped the elderly lady pick up the contents.

CAPITALIZATION:

1. does dr. partin have an office in the jefferson medical building?

PUNCTUATION:

2. On Mon Dec 21 1986 the A M A met in St Paul Minn

PARTS OF SPEECH: Verbs

3. **To + verb** is called _____.

PARTS OF SPEECH: Pronouns

       Select the correct pronoun.

4. Mary speaks more clearly than _____ (she, her).

SENTENCE COMBINING:

5. His feelings were hurt.
   Someone yelled at him.
   He won't talk to anyone.

Day 40

CAPITALIZATION:

1. have captain jones and mayor flood visited the sears tower in chicago?

PUNCTUATION:

2. Does Johns essay contain too many buts

PARTS OF SPEECH: Prepositions

Select any object of the preposition.

3. In the middle of dinner, Tom went to the store.

RUN-ONS:

Correct the run-on.

4. We'll go to the beach, Jane will drive us.

SENTENCE COMBINING:

5. Uncle Jim is a lawyer.
Susie's dad is a client of Uncle Jim.
Uncle Jim's office is downtown.

CAPITALIZATION:

1. in india, the hindu religion is the major one.

PUNCTUATION:

2. Because its raining we will stay indoors

PARTS OF SPEECH: Verbs

   Determine the tense: present, past, or future.

3. A. Bill left.
    B. Bill will go.
    C. Bill often goes there.

PARTS OF SPEECH: Adverbs

   Select any adverbs that tell **where**.

4. After we arrive home, we are going back out.

SENTENCE COMBINING:

5. That man is a custodian.
    That man is my grandfather.
    That man works at Grant School.

Day 42

CAPITALIZATION:

1. last summer the harrington twins had chicken pox.

PUNCTUATION:

2. Jill have you seen my dog the black and shaggy one

PARTS OF SPEECH: Nouns
       Write the plural form.

3. A. wherry
   B. bay
   C. neighbor
   D. glass

PARTS OF SPEECH: Prepositions
       Cross out prepositional phrases. Underline <u>subject</u> and <u>verb/verb phrase</u>.

4. Throughout the day, the ranchers had driven in their trucks.

SENTENCE COMBINING:

5. Brown sugar was stirred into the batter.
   John was making cookies.
   This was John's first time to make cookies.

CAPITALIZATION:

1. ben franklin attended the constitutional convention in philadelphia.

PUNCTUATION:

2. Although the ladies club met no decision was made

DIRECT OBJECTS:
   Select the direct object.

3. The child followed the dog along the meadow path.

PARTS OF SPEECH: Nouns
   A predicate nominative occurs in the predicate and equals the subject.
   Select the predicate nominative.

4. The last item for sale was a rocker.

SENTENCE COMBINING:

5. One pen is red, and one is green.
   The pens are on the art table.
   The pens are being used for making Christmas decorations.

Day 44

CAPITALIZATION:

1. "does jean know," asked governor brown, "that she has been elected?"

PUNCTUATION:

2. Dear Miss Lyons

   Yes Id love to visit you

       Sincerely
       Ted

PARTS OF SPEECH: Pronouns and Adjectives
Determine if **some** is a pronoun or an adjective.

3. A. We bought **some** popcorn.
   B. Will **some** be eating here?

PARTS OF SPEECH:

4. **And, but**, and **or** are called _____.

SENTENCE COMBINING:

5. The pan is greasy.
   The pan is on the stove.
   The pan is made of cast iron.
   The pan was used for frying bacon.

CAPITALIZATION:

1. our vice-president of the united states presides over the senate.

PUNCTUATION:

2. The first song in the book Worship Him is entitled We Have come into This House

PARTS OF SPEECH: Prepositions

    Cross out prepositional phrases. Underline the subject once and the verb/verb phrase twice.

3. One of the children is playing with wooden blocks.

SUBJECTS/VERBS:

    Select the correct verb.

4. A group of students (is, are) departing this afternoon.

SENTENCE COMBINING:

5. The television is broken.
   The repair person will come today.
   The television set is only two months old.

Day 46

CAPITALIZATION:

1. the plateau, sunset point, is located north of phoenix on the way to camp verde.

PUNCTUATION:

2. Yes if I am correct the answer is fifty five

PARTS OF SPEECH: Prepositions and Adverbs
        Determine if **up** is a preposition or an adverb.

3. A. Santa went **up** the chimney.
   B. We looked **up** and saw hot air balloons.

PARTS OF SPEECH:

4. What part of speech is "**WOW!**"?

SENTENCE COMBINING:

5. The cat is a Siamese.
   The cat purrs softly when stroked.

CAPITALIZATION:

1. have you ever sung the song "he shall cover me with feathers"?

PUNCTUATION:

2. In Laguna Beach California there are many beautiful hillside homes

PARTS OF SPEECH: Nouns

   Determine if the noun is abstract or concrete.

3. A. cookies
   B. honesty
   C. love
   D. air

PARTS OF SPEECH: Verbs

   Select the past participle; underline the verb phrase twice.

4. The construction workers must have _____ (broke, broken) a pipe.

SENTENCE COMBINING:

5. Abby plays tennis.
   Abby is our school champion.
   Abby will participate in a state tournament.

CAPITALIZATION:

1. the leader of the democratic party met with dad at a miami restaurant.

PUNCTUATION:

2. The Queen Mary* is in the harbor at Long Beach California

*name of ship

SENTENCE TYPES:

   Detrmine the type of sentence.

3. Take this envelope.

PARTS OF SPEECH: Verbs

   Label the tense: present, past, or future.

4. A. Mary sings in the choir.
   B. Mary will sing in the choir.
   C. The choir sang two hymns.

SENTENCE COMBINING:

5. The check was cashed.
   The check was written for $10.00.
   The teller cashed the check.

CAPITALIZATION:

1. the cape of good hope is at the southern tip of africa

PUNCTUATION:

2. The blue three tiered curtains were discarded

PARTS OF SPEECH: Verbs

3. List 10 auxiliary (helping) verbs.

PARTS OF SPEECH: Adjectives

4. Write the adjective form of the noun:
    A. beauty
    B. honesty
    C. practicality
    D. friendliness

SENTENCE COMBINING:

5. The restaurant is closed.
   The restaurant is a Chinese food restaurant.
   The restaurant will open in the morning.

Day 50

CAPITALIZATION:

1. our home is near bristol lake and mummy mountain drive.

PUNCTUATION:

2. Your warranty expires Jan 2 dont forget

PARTS OF SPEECH: Verbs

   Select the correct verb.

3. Joan _____ (sneaked, snuck) into the room.

PARTS OF SPEECH: Pronouns

   Select any possessive pronouns (used as adjectives).

4. My cat chases its tail.

SENTENCE COMBINING:

5. The cows are in the barn.
   The cows have been milked.
   The cows are black and white.

CAPITALIZATION:

1. have you been to grand central station in new york city?

PUNCTUATION:

2. The following are needed for dessert apples pie and cake

PARTS OF SPEECH: Verbs

3. List six linking verbs.

PARTS OF SPEECH: Pronouns

4. (It's, Its) in the last wagon.

SENTENCE COMBINING:

5. Many people were at the park.
   The park is located near our school.
   People were flying kites.

Day 52

CAPITALIZATION:

1. in our history book, <u>america is great</u>, we read about the <u>spirit of st. louis</u>.

PUNCTUATION:

2. Because the flour is self rising well use it

PARTS OF SPEECH: Adjective or Pronoun
Determine if **many** is used as an adjective or a pronoun.

3. A. **Many** are not traveling.
    B. **Many** tables had been set.

PHRASES/CLAUSES:
Determine if the group of words is a phrase or a clause.

4. A. After we ate lunch.
    B. After the game.

SENTENCE COMBINING:

5. The daisies are on the table.
    The daisies are fresh.
    The daisies are used as a centerpiece.

CAPITALIZATION:

1. on a chessa's choice* milk carton, you might find a coupon for eagle airlines.
*brand name

PUNCTUATION:

2. Youre to leave at 600 A M for London England

PARTS OF SPEECH: Verbs

     Determine the past participle; underline the verb phrase twice.

3. The truckers must have _____ (driven, drove) for many hours.

PARTS OF SPEECH: Pronouns

     Determine the antecedent for the possessive pronoun.

4. Mr. Tomshack gave <u>his</u> speech today.

SENTENCE COMBINING:

5. The shirt is hanging on a hanger.
   The shirt needs to be ironed.
   The shirt is blue.

Day 54

CAPITALIZATION:

1. the protestant church members met at a methodist church last sunday.

PUNCTUATION:

2. Tony asked Mother may I have some money

PARTS OF SPEECH: Verbs

3. What is the present participle of **to burst**?

PARTS OF SPEECH: Adverbs

       Choose the correct word.

4. Tom doesn't know (anything, nothing) about it.

SENTENCE COMBINING:

5. The artist painted a picture.
   The painting was of the artist's father.
   The painting won first place at the art fair.

CAPITALIZATION:

1. we visited king's world, tapa rose gardens, and the court buildings in los angeles.

PUNCTUATION:

2. Rule A Enter quietly
   Rule B Exit quietly

   Groceries
   -milk
   -eggs
   -bread

PARTS OF SPEECH: Verbs

3. Write the past tense of the infinitive **to do**.

PARTS OF SPEECH: Nouns
   Write the possessive form.

4. a club that belongs to men

SENTENCE COMBINING:

5. A tunnel went through the mountain.
   We used the tunnel.
   We had to turn on our car's headlights.

Day 56

CAPITALIZATION:

1. my mother planted japanese privets in our east garden.

PUNCTUATION:

2. Did you read an article about the Spruce Goose* in the newspaper Daily News

   *name of airplane

PARTS OF SPEECH: Nouns
        Write the possessive form.

3. a tip that belongs to a waitress

BUSINESS LETTER:
        Label the parts of a business letter.

4.
                                                    _____
                                                    _____   A.
                                                    _____

        _____   B.
        _____
        _____

        _____: C.

_____
_____   D.
_____

                                        _____,   E.
                                        _____   F.

SENTENCE COMBINING:

5. Her sister is a secretary.
   Her sister enjoys golf.
   Her sister lives in Florida.

CAPITALIZATION:

1. our class studies roman gods in our ancient literature class.

PUNCTUATION:

2. The children played the parents watched television

PARTS OF SPEECH: Pronouns
    Select the correct answer.

3. (Your, You're) bike has been found.

PARTS OF SPEECH: Adverbs

4. Write the seven adverbs that tell **to what extent** (how much).

SENTENCE COMBINING:

5. The sidewalk is slippery.
   The sidewalk is wet.
   Snow has fallen.

Day 58

CAPITALIZATION:

1. the peoria, columbus day parade marched in front of the high school.

PUNCTUATION:

2. That patient has a heart problem therefore she walks daily

PHRASES/CLAUSES:

Determine if the group of words is a phrase or a clause.

3. Running down the street.

PARTS OF SPEECH: Verbs

4. The two tenses that will never have **auxiliary** (helping) verbs are _____ and _____.

SENTENCE COMBINING:

5. Her hair is curly.
   She is tall.
   She is a model.
   She works for Baron Modeling Agency.

CAPITALIZATION:

1. the seminole indians of the south attended the conference.

PUNCTUATION:

2. In todays newspaper City Chronicle Dads picture in on p 7

PARTS OF SPEECH: Pronouns

 Select the correct pronoun.

3. Bobby and _____ (she, her) want to go.

PARTS OF SPEECH: Nouns

 Select the predicate nominative(s) in this sentence.

4. The winners of the race were Ms. Hart and Bob.

SENTENCE COMBINING:

5. A ruler was needed.
 A ruler would be used to draw a bar graph.
 The bar graph was an assignment for math.

Day 60

CAPITALIZATION:

1. i enjoy the poem, "death of a hired man," by robert frost.

PUNCTUATION:

2. Have you seen Jack any big blue balloons

PARTS OF SPEECH: Adjectives and Pronouns
        Determine if **that** is an adjective or a pronoun.

3. A. **That** is funny!
    B. **That** blouse is torn.

INDIRECT OBJECTS:
        Select the indirect object.

4. Mother has given Grandma a sweater.

SENTENCE COMBINING:

5. The tree was planted last fall.
    The tree is blossoming.
    The tree needs to be watered.

CAPITALIZATION:

1. have dr. and mrs. j. jones moved to 321 west ginger drive, el paso, texas?

PUNCTUATION:

2. Two thirds of todays math class hasnt handed in homework

PARTS OF SPEECH: Verbs

      Select the correct past participle form; underline the verb phrase twice.

3. Some students must have _____ (brought, brang) a turtle.

PARTS OF SPEECH: Pronouns

      Give the antecedent.

4. The small, quiet toddler hurt <u>his</u> knee.

SENTENCE COMBINING:

5. A crayon was left in the car.
    The crayon melted on the back seat due to the heat.
    Mother was angry.

Day 62

CAPITALIZATION:

1. some african daisies have been planted in the east garden by the mexican restaurant.

PUNCTUATION:

2. The poem entitled If was written by Rudyard Kipling a great British author

PARTS OF SPEECH: Verbs
Determine the tenses: present, past, or future.

3. A. Susan thanked me.
   B. Those bulldozers give off fumes.
   C. Mike will present his speech now.

PARTS OF SPEECH: Nouns
Write the possessive form.

4. a trophy that belongs to a class

SENTENCE COMBINING:

5. Bill drew a picture.
   Bill is in kindergarten.
   The picture showed his dog.

CAPITALIZATION:

1. some of the native americans attend an indian <u>bible</u> college.

PUNCTUATION:

2. Two thirds of the math class hasnt turned in its assignment Mary

PARTS OF SPEECH: Verbs

3. Write the present participle of the infinitive, **to finish**.

PARTS OF SPEECH: Adverbs

    Select any adverbs.

4. Tonight, we shall go there with our youth group.

SENTENCE COMBINING:

5. Lunch is served in the school cafeteria.
Lunch is pizza today.
Lunch will also include milk.

Day 64

CAPITALIZATION:

1. in june, the tompson family went to a tucson resort.

PUNCTUATION:

2. My mild mannered granny the lady in the red dress is not the culprit

PARTS OF SPEECH: Pronouns
    Select the correct pronoun.

3. Bill is taller than _____ (I, me).

PARTS OF SPEECH: Verbs
    Determine the past participle form; underline the verb phrase twice.

4. The girls had _____ (gave, given) a great performance.

SENTENCE COMBINING:

5. The boy was cold.
   The boy was shivering.
   The boy is a blonde with blue eyes.

CAPITALIZATION:

1. for breakfast, we had a danish pastry, rainmist orange juice, and a belgian waffle.

PUNCTUATION:

2. After Tates last run he struck out

PARTS OF SPEECH: Pronouns
      Select the correct answer.

3. The dog wagged _____ (it's, its) tail.

SENTENCE TYPES:

      Determine the type of sentence.

4. A. I'm going.
   B. We lost!
   C. Are you tired?
   D. Stay awake.

SENTENCE COMBINING:

5. The frog jumped into the water.
   The frog was sitting on a rock.
   The frog jumped swiftly.

Day 66

CAPITALIZATION:

1. some oriental rugs were displayed at chang's chinese furniture*.

   *name of store

PUNCTUATION:

2. On Tues Feb 28 1988 we celebrated Peters birthday

PARTS OF SPEECH: Adverbs

3. List seven adverbs that tell **to what extent** (how much).

PARTS OF SPEECH: Verbs

Select the correct form; underline the verb phrase twice.

4. The book has been _____ (chose, chosen) as an award winner.

SENTENCE COMBINING:

5. The day was hot and sunny.
   We swam in our pool.
   Mother stayed in the kitchen and baked.

CAPITALIZATION:

1. has father left the y.m.c.a. building yet?

PUNCTUATION:

2. What on earth asked Kyle are you doing

SUBJECTS/VERBS:

Underline the subject once and the verb/verb phrase twice.

3. May the students and their teacher leave now?

FRIENDLY LETTERS:

Label the parts of a friendly letter.

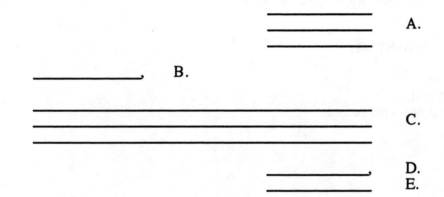

SENTENCE COMBINING:

5. The monkey was swinging from limb to limb.
   The monkey was eating a banana.
   The other monkeys watched him.

Day 68

CAPITALIZATION:

1. susan now owns flair hair care on wilson road.

PUNCTUATION:

2. We need the following lettuce ice syrup and yogurt

PARTS OF SPEECH: Verbs

3. List six linking verbs.

PARTS OF SPEECH: Nouns
      Select nouns.

4. In the middle of the assembly, they had to leave.

SENTENCE COMBINING:

5. Jane loves pizza.
   Her brother hates it.
   Jane's favorite pizza is pepperoni.

CAPITALIZATION:

1. my grandmother billings went to yosemite national park in california.

PUNCTUATION:

2. My dad the man in the red sweater is also those boys coach

PARTS OF SPEECH:

3. What part of speech is "**OH!**"?

PARTS OF SPEECH: Adjectives

      Select adjectives.

4. Those red carnations were blooming in the planter box.

SENTENCE COMBINING:

5. The blue sweater was torn.
   The sweater was torn by Jill Fox.
   The sweater was wool.

Day 70

CAPITALIZATION:

1. did you study buddhism, the religion of china and the far east?

PUNCTUATION:

2. Lilas report was entitled Mars a Great Planet

PARTS OF SPEECH: Adjectives

Write the proper adjective form for the noun.

3. A. Greece = _____food
   B. Holland= _____tulips
   C. France = _____fries
   D. Tonka = _____toys

PHRASES/CLAUSES:

Determine if the group of words is a phrase or a clause.

4. Having shut the door.

SENTENCE COMBINING:

5. The calendar is hanging on the wall.
   George Washington is pictured on the calendar.

CAPITALIZATION:

1. on monday the u. s. house of representatives discussed taxes.

PUNCTUATION:

2. The ex teacher in fact retired to Duluth Minn last summer

SENTENCE TYPES:

   Determine the type of sentence.

3. A. Prune this tree.
   B. Some will stay.
   C. Are you running?
   D. Wow! I've finished!
   E. Mary asked her aunt for skates.

PARTS OF SPEECH: Adverbs

   Select adverbs: (*how, when, where,* and *to what extent*)

4. Today, the very determined squirrel cautiously scampered away.

SENTENCE COMBINING:

5. The fitness class meets on Tuesday.
   The stamp class meets on Tuesday.
   They both meet at four o'clock.
   I have to decide to which I'll go.

Day 72

CAPITALIZATION:

1. the president of regal motor company visited a detroit factory.

PUNCTUATION:

2. Deka exclaimed the teacher you scored 100%

PARTS OF SPEECH: Pronouns

       Select the correct pronoun.

3. Catalin gave _____ (I,me) a football.

PARTS OF SPEECH: Nouns

       Write the possessive form.

4. golf clubs shared by two boys

SENTENCE COMBINING:

5. The cake is chocolate.
   The frosting is peanut butter.
   The cake is for Laylah's birthday.
   Laylah will be ten.

CAPITALIZATION:

1. we stayed at charta ski resort in fairfield, pennsylvania.

PUNCTUATION:

2. Because we are studying insects well read the chapter entitled Flying Insects

PARTS OF SPEECH: Nouns

Select the predicate nominative(s).

3. The first person in line was Tomas.

PARTS OF SPEECH: Verbs

Determine if the verb is action or linking.

4. A. The child <u>tasted</u> the soup.

B. The milk <u>tastes</u> sour.

SENTENCE COMBINING:

5. Dad went grocery shopping.
   Mom went to her office.
   I shall play tennis.

Day 74

CAPITALIZATION:

1. an army lieutenant purchased po queen* vegetables for a chinese party.
*brand name

PUNCTUATION:

2. Kaleena Drang D D S will speak about decay plaque and flossing

PARTS OF SPEECH: Pronouns

  Give the pronoun antecedent.

3. Some hamsters played in <u>their</u> cages.

PARTS OF SPEECH: Nouns

4. Words ending with ____, ____, ____, ____, and ____ add *es* to form the plural.

SENTENCE COMBINING:

5. Art class was held outside.
   Students sketched a landscape.
   Most students enjoyed the class.

CAPITALIZATION:

1. the battle of shiloh, fought during the civil war, is described in our american history book.

PUNCTUATION:

2. Larrys sculpture is the tall curved one

PARTS OF SPEECH: Nouns
       Write the plural of the nouns.

3. A. calf
   B. mustard
   C. mouse
   D. grief
   E. loss

PARTS OF SPEECH: Conjunctions

4. Write the three common conjunctions.

SENTENCE COMBINING:

5. "Mary had a little lamb.
   Its fleece was white as snow.
   Everywhere that Mary went, her lamb was sure to go."

Day 76

CAPITALIZATION:

1. during elizabethan times, william shakespeare wrote the play, <u>a midsummer night's dream</u>.

PUNCTUATION:

2. Dear Jan

Ill see you on Monday Dec 5th 2005 at 200 P M

PARTS OF SPEECH: Pronouns and Adjectives
Determine if the word serves as a pronoun or an adjective.

3. A. **Many** bookmarks were ordered.
   B. Are **many** eligible?
   C. I like **that** watch.
   D. I like **that**!

SENTENCE TYPES:
Determine the sentence type.

4. A. It's time!
   B. Stop.
   C. Will you stop?
   D. The rain has slackened.

SENTENCE COMBINING:

5. The flowers were orchids.
   The flowers formed a bouquet.
   The bouquet was for the bride.
   The bouquet was lovely.

CAPITALIZATION:

1. "ode to a grecian urn" wasn't written by john donne.

PUNCTUATION:

2. The C H Jobe Co moved to 24 Bilt St Lincoln Neb

PARTS OF SPEECH: Adjectives
        Select the predicate adjective(s) in the sentence.

3. Her voice was hoarse from yelling.

PHRASES/CLAUSES:
        Determine if the clause is independent or dependent.

4. When she was young.

SENTENCE COMBINING:

5. John won a prize.
    He was the outstanding salesperson in his company.
    The prize was a trip to Hawaii.

Day 78

CAPITALIZATION:

1. the polio vaccine, also called the salk vaccine after dr. jonas salk, was being given at st. jerome's hospital.

PUNCTUATION:

2. The story All Summer in a Day was read by Mrs Larks class

PARTS OF SPEECH: Pronouns

Select the correct pronoun that agrees with the antecedent.

3. Some speakers gave _____ (his, their) presentations.

PARTS OF SPEECH: Nouns

Select nouns.

4. The majority of voters asked for a recall of the official.

SENTENCE COMBINING:

5. The baby was given a pink stuffed bunny.
   The gift was for Easter.
   The baby laughed and chewed on the bunny's ear.

CAPITALIZATION:

1. my sister, anita, speaks arabic and studies iranian customs.

PUNCTUATION:

2. This spot quiet and secluded is my favorite said Jim

PARTS OF SPEECH: Nouns
    Write the possessive form.

3. a toy that belongs to all the babies

PARTS OF SPEECH: Verbs
    Select the verb that agrees with the subject.

4. Those dentists (come, comes) here daily.

SENTENCE COMBINING:

5. The students are studying World War I.
   The students are doing projects.
   Some students are writing research papers.

Day 80

CAPITALIZATION:

1. during james monroe's office, there was an "era of good feeling."

PUNCTUATION:

2. Basketball isnt difficult but Id rather play tennis

PHRASES/CLAUSES:

Determine if the clause is independent or dependent.

3. Although the snow had ceased.

SUBJECTS/VERBS:

Underline the subject once and the verb/verb phrase twice.

4. Under the tree near the town square sat a man with his dog.

SENTENCE COMBINING:

5. We sat on a rock.
   We were throwing pebbles into a lake.
   A train sped by.

CAPITALIZATION:

1. the german language teacher is ill with the asian flu.

PUNCTUATION:

2. If youre going bring half of the food

PARTS OF SPEECH: Adverbs

　　　Underline the two negatives. Rewrite the sentence correctly.

3. He didn't have no money.

INDIRECT OBJECTS:

　　　Select the indirect object(s).

4. For Valentine's Day, Dad gave Mom a box of candy.

SENTENCE COMBINING:

5. Measles is a childhood disease.
   Tim has measles.
   Tim will not be in school.

Day 82

CAPITALIZATION:

1. while in san francisco, we crossed the golden gate bridge.

PUNCTUATION:

2. The article entitled Food Funds appeared in the newspaper The Star Republic

PARTS OF SPEECH: Pronouns
   Select the pronoun that serves as a predicate nominative.

3. With us, the first choice will be you.

PARTS OF SPEECH: Adjectives
   Select adjectives.

4. A soft breeze calmly blew in the early morning.

SENTENCE COMBINING:

5. We visited San Diego.
   We went sailing.
   We also went fishing and surfing.

CAPITALIZATION:

1. the cape of good hope is at the southern tip of africa.

PUNCTUATION:

2. Deana remarked I like the mountains in Virginia

PARTS OF SPEECH: Adverbs
      Select any adverbs.

3. Yesterday we didn't leave early for lunch.

PARTS OF SPEECH: Pronouns and Adjectives
      Determine if the word is used as a pronoun or adjective.

4. A. **Those** need to be ironed.
    B. **That** briefcase is mine.
    C. You may take **several**.

SENTENCE COMBINING:

5. The car was parked.
   The car was at the bottom of the hill.
   The car had been abandoned.
   The car had been stolen.

Day 84

CAPITALIZATION:

1. when captain hale visited the grand canyon, he met some japanese tourists.

PUNCTUATION:

2. Sally I dont have any replied the mother

PHRASES/CLAUSES

3. A _____ (clause, phrase) always contains a subject and verb.

PARTS OF SPEECH: Verbs

      Select the verb that agrees with the subject.

4. Many nails (have, has) been used.

SENTENCE COMBINING:

5. John visited Peru.
   He enjoyed the Andes Mountains.
   John wants to return again next summer.

CAPITALIZATION:

1. the movie, lady and the tramp, was playing at fox theater.

PUNCTUATION:

2. Ellen Smith D D S has her office in the Tracton Building

PHRASES/CLAUSES:

      Determine if the group of words is a phrase or a clause.

3. Nut bread is in the oven.

PARTS OF SPEECH: Pronouns

      Choose the correct pronoun.

4. Those hikers travel faster than _____ (us, we).

SENTENCE COMBINING:

5. There were miniature music boxes for sale.
    They were made of porcelain.
    They were edged in gold.

Day 86

CAPITALIZATION:

1. during labor day weekend, we went to an eastern university. *

   *a university in the East, a region of the country

PUNCTUATION:

2. Theyre absolutely right however Prof Lee may disagree

PARTS OF SPEECH: Prepositions

   Select any object of the preposition.

3. The group of vacationers fished from the Oregon coast down to San Diego.

PARTS OF SPEECH: Verbs

   Determine the verb tense.

4. A. The team **dives** daily.
   B. Joe **fought** a cold.
   C. I **shall play** the piano.

SENTENCE COMBINING:

5. Karen's parents are vegetarians.
   Karen's parents don't eat any meat.
   Karen enjoys hot dogs.

CAPITALIZATION:

1. is golton's tea or columbian coffee served at hungry-boy restaurant?

PUNCTUATION:

2. Jess havent you met Mr Cline the dance instructor

PARTS OF SPEECH: Nouns

     Write the possessive form.

3. a bowl shared by two dogs

PARTS OF SPEECH: Adjectives

     Select the correct form.

4. Of our three horses, this one is (more gentle, most gentle).

SENTENCE COMBINING:

5. The pancakes were blueberry.
   The pancakes were burned.
   The toast was also burned.
   The eggs were soggy.

Day 88

CAPITALIZATION:

1. chris and i took flax taxi service to the john wayne international airport in orange county, calif.

PUNCTUATION:

2. On June 7 1995 my parents visited Idaho Ohio and Utah

PARTS OF SPEECH: Verbs
  Write the contraction.

3. A. cannot
   B. will not
   C. do not
   D. I had
   E. she will

PARTS OF SPEECH: Adjectives
  Select adjectives.

4. My old, rusted bike was painted a bright green color.

SENTENCE COMBINING:

5. Her suit was wool.
   Her suit was pin-striped.
   Her suit was made in England.
   Her suit was purchased for a business conference.

CAPITALIZATION:

1. our class studied the mayflower compact and the pilgrims' beginnings in america.

PUNCTUATION:

2. Theres no t in pebble said the teacher

PARTS OF SPEECH: Adverbs

3. Write the superlative form of **dangerously**.

PARTS OF SPEECH: Verbs

4. Write the present participle of **to fly**.

SENTENCE COMBINING:

5. We are going skiing.
   Then, we are going sledding.
   Then, we are going ice skating.

Day 90

CAPITALIZATION:

1. sugar cookies and castaway's corn flakes were bought at kosey's cafe.

PUNCTUATION:

2. When the cars red light came on Jamilah stopped

PARTS OF SPEECH: Prepositions and Adverbs
    Determine if the word is a preposition or an adverb.

3. A. **Out** into the darkness he fled.
   B. Dad rushed **out** the door.
   C. Come **in** through the garage.
   D. Your puzzle is **in** the attic.

PARTS OF SPEECH: Nouns
    Write the plural.

4. A. movie   B. lady   C. monkey   D. proof   E. mother-in-law

SENTENCE COMBINING:

5. The nurses administer medication.
   The nurses work long hours.
   They consult with the doctors.

CAPITALIZATION:

1. i. great battles
        a. american victories
           1. naval battles
           2. skirmishes on land
        b. triumphs of the british

PUNCTUATION:

2. I wont go Tammy please stay with me

PARTS OF SPEECH: Adverbs
    Select any adverbs.

3. We already had completed nearly three laps together.

FRIENDLY LETTERS: Letter parts
    Label the letter parts.

4.

                                        A.

                 ,   B.

                                    C.

                         ,   D.
                                    E.

SENTENCE COMBINING:

5. My birthday is next week.
    Grandpa usually sends money.
    Mom usually makes my favorite meal.

CAPITALIZATION:

1. the story entitled "days of our serenity" was read in english class.

PUNCTUATION:

2. Mrs Hester L Strong
   222 E Irvine Blvd
   Tustin CA

PARTS OF SPEECH: Pronouns

3. Write an example of a reflexive pronoun.

PARTS OF SPEECH: Adjectives

   Select the correct adjective form.

4. This puppy is the (more adorable, most adorable) of the two.

SENTENCE COMBINING:

5. The toy won't work.
   The toy is a truck.
   The batteries are dead.
   There are new batteries in the drawer.

CAPITALIZATION:

1. my dear friend,

     see me at tomorrow's hispanic fair.

          yours truly,
          sean

PUNCTUATION:

2. Whos the author of the poem The Raven

PARTS OF SPEECH: Verbs

3. Another name for a helping verb is an _____ verb.

SUBJECTS/VERBS:

     Underline the subject once and the verb/verb phrase twice.

4. Some robins perched on the fountain and flew suddenly away.

SENTENCE COMBINING:

5. Mia is a baby.
Mia has four teeth.
Mia bites her brother.
Her brother just laughs.

Day 94

CAPITALIZATION:

1. the <u>u.s.s. constitution</u>,* now in boston harbor, was used in the war of 1812.

    *name of ship

PUNCTUATION:

2. Running down the street the dog knocked over Marks bike

PARTS OF SPEECH: Pronouns
        Select the correct form.

3. The speaker will be _____ (she, her).

PARTS OF SPEECH: Verbs

4. List the 23 auxiliary (helping) verbs.

SENTENCE COMBINING:

5. The floor tile is cracked.
    The tile is from Italy
    The tile has geometric designs.
    The tile needs to be replaced.

CAPITALIZATION:

1. the sixth grade performed a thanksgiving play called <u>of pilgrims we are proud</u>.

PUNCTUATION:

2. Armistice Day also known as Veterans Day is Nov 11

SUBJECTS/VERBS:

      Underline the subject once and the verb/verb phrase twice.

3. A balloon had drifted from her hand and was soaring upward.

DIRECT OBJECTS:

      Determine if the word is a direct object.

4. A. She put her **cup** in the sink.
   B. I don't feel **well**.
   C. My coach is Russ's **dad**.
   D. The police searched the **room**.

SENTENCE COMBINING:

5. A siren sounded shrill.
An ambulance sped by our house.
The siren woke us.

Day 96

CAPITALIZATION:

1. we toured holuba hall during our summer visit to penn state university.

PUNCTUATION:

2. The low rolling hills were a photographers dream remarked Marion

PARTS OF SPEECH: Nouns

What is the underlined noun phrase called?

3. The decorations, <u>hearts and flowers,</u> were used for the dance.

PARTS OF SPEECH: Adverbs

4. Write the superlative form of **well**.

SENTENCE COMBINING:

5. The golfers met at 6 A.M.
   The course was already filled.
   The golfers decided to try another golf course.

CAPITALIZATION:

1. <u>the great gatsby</u> is an american literature book by fitzgerald.

PUNCTUATION:

2. Susan take this for me I need to leave now

SUBJECTS/VERBS:

      Underline the subject once and the verb/verb phrase twice.

3. Many of the apples had not been eaten.

PARTS OF SPEECH: Adverbs

4. Write the comparative form of **slowly**.

SENTENCE COMBINING:

5. The flowers are blooming.
    The flowers are red and white petunias.
    They were planted two months ago.

Day 98

CAPITALIZATION:

1. the mclean family attends a lutheran church in albany, new york.

PUNCTUATION:

2. We will meet without a doubt to discuss Mrs Smiths account

SUBJECTS/VERBS:

3. The ducks and birds are enjoying the spring day.

PARTS OF SPEECH: Pronouns
         Give the antecedent.

4. The ladies have purchased <u>their</u> tickets.

SENTENCE COMBINING:

5. My aunt is a dental hygienist.
    My aunt cleans my teeth.
    My aunt recommends that I brush more often.

Day 99

CAPITALIZATION:

1. during the fall, we will visit the university of florida and the jacksonville naval air station.

PUNCTUATION:

2. At 915 A M on Sept 7 Ill see the movie Tiger Eyes

PARTS OF SPEECH: Verbs
Determine the tense.

3. A. He **will jump** now.
   B. Friends **are** forever.
   C. It **lasted** too long.

PARTS OF SPEECH: Nouns
Determine if the word is a concrete or abstract noun.

4. A. patience
   B. bitterness
   C. dust

SENTENCE COMBINING:

5. We went to the zoo.
   We enjoyed the giraffes the most.
   Our class went last week.

Day 100

CAPITALIZATION:

1. a lieutenant with the st. paul police dept. spoke about self-defense.

PUNCTUATION:

2. His brother in law works in Topeka Kansas twice a year

PARTS OF SPEECH: Verbs

      Select the past participle form; underline the verb phrase twice.

3. Has someone (rode, ridden) the bus?

PARTS OF SPEECH: Prepositions

      Determine the object(s) of each preposition.

4. During the storm, several trees fell by the side of the road.

SENTENCE COMBINING:

5. Our scout troop meets Wednesday.
   Mr. and Mrs. Burns are our leaders.
   They invited Deputy Jones to speak.
   Deputy Jones will speak on desert survival.

CAPITALIZATION:

1. is the <u>queen anne</u> a british or an american ocean liner?

PUNCTUATION:

2. The childs shoe broke her mother repaired it

DIRECT OBJECTS/ INDIRECT OBJECTS:

Select the direct object and the indirect object.

3. The coach gave them a pep talk.

PARTS OF SPEECH: Nouns

Write a proper noun for each common noun.

4. A. boy
   B. school
   C. restaurant

SENTENCE COMBINING:

5. Rain fell heavily.
   The roads were filled with deep puddles.
   There was also a cold wind blowing.

CAPITALIZATION:

1. the strait of gibraltar and the suez canal are gateways to the mediterranean sea.

PUNCTUATION:

2. Didnt her name appear on the list as Markle Susan

PARTS OF SPEECH: Verbs

      Select the verb; underline the verb phrase twice.

3. The burglar might have _____ (sneaked, snuck) into the office.

PARTS OF SPEECH: Pronouns

      Select the correct pronoun.

4. May the others and _____ (I, me) decide?

SENTENCE COMBINING:

5. The trees were covered with snow.
   The trees were pine.
   Snow had fallen throughout the night.

CAPITALIZATION:

1. at gore meadow school, ms. jones teaches "the midnight ride of paul revere" in her reading class.

PUNCTUATION:

2. Your decision Im afraid will create lasting problems

PARTS OF SPEECH: Pronouns

       Determine if the pronoun is a direct object, indirect object, or object of the preposition.

3. A. They took **us** home.
   B. Ken has given **them** a flag.
   C. May I sit near **you**?

PARTS OF SPEECH: Adjectives

       Select adjectives.

4. Some loaded fishing boats anchored on the luminous, deep water.

SENTENCE COMBINING:

5. Squirrels scampered in the forest.
   They gathered nuts.
   They stored them in a tree.
   They were suddenly frightened by voices in the forest.

Day 104

CAPITALIZATION:

1. the french toast is served on bavarian plates at duck and delight diner.

PUNCTUATION:

2. When the childrens playground is finished lets go there

PARTS OF SPEECH: Nouns
       Write the possessive form.

3. a pet belonging to Sue and Tom

PARTS OF SPEECH: Adjectives
       Select adjectives.

4. The fallen leaves, brown and crisp, smelled fragrant.

SENTENCE COMBINING:

5. An alligator lives in Okefenokee Swamp.
   The alligator showed his teeth.
   The reason the alligator did this was to warn an intruder.

CAPITALIZATION:

1. one of the french artists, manet, entitled his work <u>brioche with pears</u>.

PUNCTUATION:

2. Susan Lang a German born citizen spoke at our riders club meeting

PARTS OF SPEECH: Verbs
     Write the tense.

3. A. Sal **eats** rapidly.
   B. **Will** you **allow** me to ask?
   C. Lyle **passed** his test.

FRIENDLY LETTERS:
     Label the parts.

4.

                                                          _____
                                                          _____   A.
                                                          _____

_____,   B.

_____
_____   C.
_____

                                                        _____,   D.
                                                        _____   E.

SENTENCE COMBINING:

5. A feather bed is like a huge pillow.
   It conforms to your body.
   Cousin Gwen bought me one during her vacation in Europe.

Day 106

CAPITALIZATION:

1. were the comanche indians led by chief parker allowed to stay on an oklahoma reservation?

PUNCTUATION:

2. In the book Silas Marner was the misers life self indulgent

PARTS OF SPEECH: Adjectives or Adverbs
Determine if the boldfaced word is an adjective or adverb.

3. A. Jane walks **slowly**.
    B. Jane is a **slow** walker.
    C. Bob drew it **better**.
    D. He's a **better** swimmer than I.

PHRASES/CLAUSES:
Label **IC** for independent clause and **DC** for dependent clause.

4. A. After we went to the game.
    B. I'm hiking soon.
    C. Although we were correct.
    D. Jane's dad is a mason.

SENTENCE COMBINING:

5. Marv's eye is bloodshot.
    Marv has an eye infection
    Marv's eye is swollen, also.

CAPITALIZATION:

1. is the minister of park presbyterian church on blake street a pastor smith?

PUNCTUATION:

2. Millie said Janes brother in law wasnt re elected as governor

PARTS OF SPEECH: Pronouns

      Select the correct pronoun.

3. The book was given to my brother and _____ (I, me).

SUBJECTS/VERBS:

      Underline the subject once and the verb/verb phrase twice.

4. One of the farmers had planted his crops and is hoping for rain.

SENTENCE COMBINING:

5. The class president was elected today.
   Sue won.
   I voted for Ted.

Day 108

CAPITALIZATION:

1. in the article entitled "religions of the world," some israelite leaders and hindu beliefs were discussed.

PUNCTUATION:

2. On Fri Sept 8 Tom and Alices stories will be read on television at 8 A M

PARTS OF SPEECH: Adjective or Pronoun

Determine if the boldfaced word serves as an adjective or pronoun.

3. A. He bought **several** pants.
   B. **Several** of the cats purred.
   C. **Several** crews had finished.

PARTS OF SPEECH: Adverbs

Correct this sentence.

4. The child never wants none.

SENTENCE COMBINING:

5. The telephone was knocked off the hook.
   The telephone is in the kitchen and is blue.
   There was a beeping sound coming from it.

CAPITALIZATION:

1. i gave valentines to my friends on st. valentine's day last february.

PUNCTUATION:

2. Marie said Mother may I go to the dance

PARTS OF SPEECH: Adverbs
     Select the correct word.

3. Martha sings _____ (loud, loudly).

PARTS OF SPEECH: Verbs

4. List the 23 auxiliary verbs (helping verbs).

SENTENCE COMBINING:

5. Mrs. Kerr is president of P.T.A.
     Mindy is her daughter.
     Mindy is in fourth grade.
     Mrs. Kerr was named outstanding leader.

Day 110

CAPITALIZATION:

1. at the st. paul's winter carnival,* you will see ice palaces.

    *name of particular carnival

PUNCTUATION:

2. A spacious elegant lobby opened onto a well lighted veranda

FRIENDLY LETTER:

3/4. Write a brief, friendly letter. Include a formal heading.

SENTENCE COMBINING:

5. The envelopes are in the desk drawer.
    The stamps are in there, also.
    Put the stamps on the envelopes.
    Mail the envelopes.

CAPITALIZATION:

1. the ship, <u>james and mary</u>, was a british one located at royal dockyard.*

   *name of particular shipyard

PUNCTUATION:

2. Youre without a doubt the teams best player exclaimed Ned

PARTS OF SPEECH: Verbs
   Write the verb.

3. A. past tense of **to fall**
   B. present tense of **to do**
   C. past tense of **to choose**
   D. future tense of **to run**

PARTS OF SPEECH: Prepositions
   Select the object(s) of each preposition.

4. The papers on the floor and sofa will be put into the trash.

SENTENCE COMBINING:

5. The sign is black and white.
   It is a large one.
   It says, "Sal's Pizzeria."
   The sign is lighted after dark.

Day 112

CAPITALIZATION:

1. our scout troop attended an independence day celebration at lake powell.

PUNCTUATION:

2. If you cross your ts in the word letter youll have a perfect paper Paul

PARTS OF SPEECH:
Determine if the noun is **common** or **proper**.

3. A. BANANA
   B. CANARY
   C. MUMMY MOUNTAIN
   D. OCEAN
   E. MILL HOSPITAL

PARTS OF SPEECH:

4. What part of speech is **"WOW!"**?

SENTENCE COMBINING:

5. Sharon broke her fingernail.
   She was pulling a staple from her paper.
   She cried out in disgust.

CAPITALIZATION:

1. the tory party was a political one during the american revolution.

PUNCTUATION:

2. Were going into the teachers lounge for a workbook

PARTS OF SPEECH: Pronouns
    Select the correct pronoun; give the antecedent.

3. Several trees shed (its, their) leaves.

PARTS OF SPEECH: Adverbs and Prepositions
    Determine if the boldfaced word is an adverb or a preposition.

4. A. The audience sat **down**.
   B. **Down** the street galloped the horse.
   C. I fell **down** into a hole.

SENTENCE COMBINING:

5. Pliers lay on the workbench.
   Various tools were lying on the floor.
   Karen is in the midst of making furniture again.

Day 114

CAPITALIZATION:

1. have you ever visited the tropical garden zoo on seventh street?

PUNCTUATION:

Punctuate the parts of a friendly letter.

2.   27 Poe Rd
                                       Columbus Ohio
                                       May 7 2009

Dear Bob
     Ill send you the book Tex soon
                                       Your friend
                                       Janet

PARTS OF SPEECH: Adjectives

Select the correct form.

3. Gloria is the (luckier, luckiest) twin.

PARTS OF SPEECH: Conjunctions

Select the correlative conjunctions.

4. Either the bird exhibit or the monkey one is my favorite.

SENTENCE COMBINING:

5. The team ran onto the field.
   The crowd cheered.
   The crowd also stood.
   The team hoped for a victory.

CAPITALIZATION:

1.
77 dree st.
san diego, ca
june 2, 2009

to my best friend,
    i will met you at kennedy international airport.
                love always,
                mickey

PUNCTUATION:

2. Is Capt Kirk aboard the Enterprise on the television show Star Trek

PARTS OF SPEECH: Verbs
Select the correct past participle; determine the verb phrase.

3. Has your aunt _____ (come, came) to visit?

PARTS OF SPEECH: Pronouns
Select the correct pronoun.

4. The next speakers are Ms. Tils and _____ (me, I).

SENTENCE COMBINING:

5. A tractor is in Uncle Ted's barn.
A red sports car is beside it.
Uncle Ted enjoys driving both.

CAPITALIZATION:

1. i. furniture
      a. beds
         1. types of beds
         2. care of beds
      b. chairs
   ii. belongings

PUNCTUATION:

2. The M C Kraft Co has moved to 33 Trellis Dr St Louis Missouri

PARTS OF SPEECH:

Select adjectives.

3. Our favorite uncle works hard as a creative writer.

SUBJECTS/VERBS:

Underline the subject once and the verb/verb phrase twice.

4. Should Bill or his family have gone so early?

SENTENCE COMBINING:

5. The gift was wrapped in red foil.
   The red foil was shiny.
   A bow was placed on the gift.
   The bow was pink taffeta.
   Three red lollipops were gathered in the bow.

CAPITALIZATION:

1. jo ellen studied southwest indian culture at a university in latin america.

PUNCTUATION:

2. At 200 P M I need the following paint three brushes and two rollers

PARTS OF SPEECH: Pronouns

3. List the nominative pronouns that serve as subject or predicate nominative.

PARTS OF SPEECH: Adverbs
   Select adverbs.

4. Yesterday, you arrived quite late for the meeting.

SENTENCE COMBINING:

5. The basket was filled with dried flowers.
   There were pine cones in the bottom.
   The basket was small and was wicker.

Day 118

CAPITALIZATION:

1. after a lunch at a nagasaki* restaurant, we visited a shinto temple in japan.

   *name of city

PUNCTUATION:
Use underline or quotation marks.

2. A. a play, Hamlet
   B. a poem, If
   C. a book, Marie
   D. a chapter, Westward Ho

SUBJECTS/VERBS:
Underline the subject once and the verb/verb phrase twice.

3. Both the play and the story were good.

PHRASES/CLAUSES:
Is the group of words a phrase or a clause?

4. Standing in line.

SENTENCE COMBINING:

5. The toddlers played in the mud.
   They made mud pies.
   They smeared mud on the wall.
   They enjoyed the soft and mushy mud.

CAPITALIZATION:

1. in greek literature, we studied gods like ares and goddesses like athena.

PUNCTUATION:

2. This idea in fact said Bob wasnt suggested

SUBJECTS/VERBS:

Underline the subject once and the verb/verb phrase twice.

3. Did the cook, the waiter, or the hostess lose the check?

SENTENCE TYPES:

Determine the sentence type.

4. A. Is it two?
   B. Water the plants, please.
   C. Dinner is served.
   D. No! I won't!

SENTENCE COMBINING:

5. Rain had fallen for two days.
   The streets were flooded.
   The river was overflowing.

Day 120

CAPITALIZATION:

1. the first ruling family of china was the hsia dynasty.

PUNCTUATION:

2. Her mother in law the lady in the pink blouse is Joan Davis R N

PARTS OF SPEECH: Pronouns
        Select the correct pronoun.

3. George sings more loudly than _____ (me, I).

SENTENCE/FRAGMENT/RUN-ON:
        Determine if the group of words is a sentence, a fragment, or a run-on.

4. Because of the extensive training, do well in field and track.

SENTENCE COMBINING:

5. Jill watched television.
   Her sister read a book.
   Her mother talked on the phone.

CAPITALIZATION:

1. in our seventh grade english class, we read "gift of the magi" by o. henry.

PUNCTUATION:

   Use underlining or quotation marks.

2. A. the airplane, Spruce Goose
   B. the nursery rhyme, Jack and Jill
   C. the magazine, Health and Wealth
   D. the magazine article, Food to You

PARTS OF SPEECH: Adverbs

   Select the correct form.

3. Does Yancy speak _____ (slow, slowly)?

PARTS OF SPEECH: Verbs

4. Write the auxiliary (helping) verbs.

SENTENCE COMBINING:

5. We went to a carnival.
   We saw a clown.
   The clown made funny animals from balloons.
   The carnival is held annually.

Day 122

CAPITALIZATION:

Capitalize the following titles.

1. A. "a walk in the park"
   B. "the yellow rose of texas"
   C. <u>i know what you did last summer</u>
   D. <u>one flew over the cuckoo's nest</u>

PUNCTUATION:

2. Lifes pleasures are exciting at age forty two said Lieut Hine

PARTS OF SPEECH: Nouns

Select any nouns.

3. Some puppies rolled over on their backs, slipped off the rug, and yelped.

PARTS OF SPEECH: Pronouns

Select the correct pronoun.

4. The composer gave the music to Ms. Sims and _____ (I, me).

SENTENCE COMBINING:

5. The children waited patiently for their dad.
   Their dad was getting dressed.
   Their dad had promised to take them for ice cream.

CAPITALIZATION:

1. will you, mother, ask senator jobe to take us on a tour of the u. s. senate in washington, d. c.?

PUNCTUATION:

2. The book Designed by God discusses a womans life

PARTS OF SPEECH: Pronouns

Make the possessive agree with the antecedent.

3. Everyone left (their, his) belongings.

PARTS OF SPEECH: Verbs

Select the correct past participle; underline the verb phrase twice.

4. Has anyone _____ (rode, ridden) this horse?

SENTENCE COMBINING:

5. The girl fell during the race.
   The girl sprained her ankle.
   The girl could not finish.

Day 124

CAPITALIZATION:

1. the organization of american states* is a central american group.

    *name of particular organization

PUNCTUATION:

2. The boss the coworker and Joans father attended the meeting

PARTS OF SPEECH: Preposition or Adverb
Determine if the boldfaced word serves as a preposition or as an adverb.

3. A. Stand **near**.
    B. I live **near** Omaha.
    C. The ape drew **near** to me.

PARTS OF SPEECH: Adjectives
Select any adjectives.

4. A serious remark was made about archaeological findings.

SENTENCE COMBINING:

5. A butterfly fluttered on the patio.
    The butterfly was yellow and black.
    A bee also buzzed by.

CAPITALIZATION:

1. during the renaissance, johann gutenberg produced a typed book.

PUNCTUATION:

2. Sen Barkins address is 21 Dale Ln Houston Texas in the summer

PARTS OF SPEECH: Nouns

Select any possessive nouns in the sentence.

3. Sue's sweater is in the school's cafeteria.

PHRASES/CLAUSES:

Determine if the group of words is a phrase or a clause.

4. A. Throughout the day.
   B. Our job is finished.
   C. Although the bus left.

SENTENCE COMBINING:

5. The vest was stained with mustard.
   It was John's vest.
   John had spilled mustard from his hot dog.

Day 126

CAPITALIZATION:

1. the french protestants were called huguenots.

PUNCTUATION:

2. I havent any time now but lets meet at Toms house later

PARTS OF SPEECH: Nouns
        Write the plural form.

3. A. moose
    B. supply
    C. commander in chief
    D. goose
    E. flash

PARTS OF SPEECH: Verbs
        Select the verb that agrees with the subject.

4. Monkeys (climb, climbs) in that tree daily.

SENTENCE COMBINING:

5. Apples hang on the trees.
   The apples are red and juicy.
   The apples need to be picked.
   The apples are in danger of rotting.

CAPITALIZATION:

1. the graduation ceremonies at blake junior high school will be in harman hall.

PUNCTUATION:

Punctuate the following titles.

2. A. a television show, Wheel of Fortune
   B. a story, Millie
   C. a magazine article, Hair Care

PARTS OF SPEECH: Nouns

3. Write one example of an abstract noun and one of a concrete noun.

PARTS OF SPEECH: Verbs

Select the past participle; underline the verb phrase twice.

4. The nail was _____ (drove, driven) in.

SENTENCE COMBINING:

5. A yellow pen lay on the table.
   The pen was broken.
   Marlo had used it to write a report.

Day 128

CAPITALIZATION:

1. the girl who joined girl scout troop 74 lives near garden grove freeway.

PUNCTUATION:

2. A news update revealed that Gov Doe had a two thirds majority

PARTS OF SPEECH: Adverbs

3. Write the seven adverbs that tell **to what extent**.

SUBJECTS/VERBS:

> Underline the subject once and the verb/verb phrase twice.

4. Both of the skaters fell and quickly arose.

SENTENCE COMBINING:

5. Mountains were tall and majestic.
    Sunshine shone on them.
    Snow covered the mountain peaks.

CAPITALIZATION:

1. does the famous skyline drive run east of the appalachian mountains?

PUNCTUATION:

2. This isnt the recipes amount you need one third cup of butter

DIRECT OBJECTS/INDIRECT OBJECTS:
   Label the direct object and the indirect object.

3. The boy gave his sister a puppy.

PARTS OF SPEECH: Nouns
   Select any nouns.

4. The beauty and serenity of this place is truly a wonder.

SENTENCE COMBINING:

5. Our daisies are blooming.
   The spring weather has been favorable.
   Last week's rain helped.

Day 130

CAPITALIZATION:

1. the hopi indians who live in the southwest* make lovely jewelry.

    *name of a particular region

PUNCTUATION:

2. An article Braille on the Trail appeared in the magazine Hiking Adventures

PARTS OF SPEECH: Verbs

3. List six linking verbs.

PARTS OF SPEECH: Adjectives
        Select any adjectives.

4. A gracious restaurant hostess showed us to a secluded table.

SENTENCE COMBINING:

5. The light is burned out.
   The light is in the hallway.
   The light has not worked for two weeks.
   I will change the bulb.

CAPITALIZATION:

1. has the "rhyme of the ancient mariner" been introduced in your junior high class?

PUNCTUATION:

2. After weve been to the store well eat lunch rest and golf

PARTS OF SPEECH: Verbs

3. List the **23** auxiliary (helping) verbs.

PARTS OF SPEECH: Diagramming
  Diagram this sentence.

4. Some ponies galloped across the field.

SENTENCE COMBINING:

5. Construction began on the home.
   The cement was poured.
   The carpenters will start tomorrow.

Day 132

CAPITALIZATION:

1. dawn's siamese cat had been found by officer dobb last monday.

PUNCTUATION:

2. Miss James asked Why arent we finished class

PARTS OF SPEECH: Adverbs

      Select any adverbs.

3. Suddenly a rather old squirrel rushed out of the tree and ran away.

PARTS OF SPEECH: Verbs

      Write the present, past, and past participle of the infinitives.

4. A. to drink
   B. to freeze
   C. to know

SENTENCE COMBINING:

5. A toy lay on the living room floor.
   The toddler had dropped it to play with a puzzle.
   The mother stumbled over the toy.

CAPITALIZATION:

1. the dree middle school was open on presidents' day but not for memorial day.

PUNCTUATION:

2. In March 1990 we moved to Dads hometown Nashville Tenn

PARTS OF SPEECH: Pronouns
   Select the correct pronoun.

3. Has anyone seen Kit and _____ (he, him)?

PARTS OF SPEECH: Verbs

4. The present participle of **to walk** is _____.

SENTENCE COMBINING:

5. The child had fallen from a tree.
   The child had broken his arm.
   The child had visited a hospital.
   A doctor had put a cast on the arm.

Day 134

CAPITALIZATION:

1. "is anyone," asked congressman pedd, "having an arbor day celebration?"

PUNCTUATION:

2. No we wont stay and Im without a doubt relieved

PARTS OF SPEECH: Pronouns
   Determine the possessive pronoun; then, determine its antecedent.

3. The scuba diver had chosen her partner.

PARTS OF SPEECH: Adjectives
   Select any adjectives.

4. The man, angry and trembling, yelled at that motorist.

SENTENCE COMBINING:

5. The runners were excited about the race.
   The race was a relay.
   Classes competed for a trophy.

CAPITALIZATION:

1. the swimming club met at the jewish community center* in eastern dallas.

   *name of particular center

PUNCTUATION:

2. Rule A NO HITTING
   Rule B NO SHOVING

PARTS OF SPEECH: Verbs
   Give the present, past, and past participle of the following infinitives.

3. A. to go
   B. to lie (rest)
   C. to burst

SENTENCE TYPES:

4. Give an example of an imperative sentence.

SENTENCE COMBINING:

5. The sea gull glided over the ocean.
   The sea gull swooped low over the beach.
   The sea gull landed on a jagged rock.

CAPITALIZATION:

Capitalize the following titles.

1. A. "raindrops keep falling on my head"
   B. everything is negotiable
   C. "don't sit under the apple tree with anyone else but me"

PUNCTUATION:

2. Our principal Tom Nast makes short snappy speeches

PARTS OF SPEECH: Nouns

Write the possessive form.

3. a book belonging to the twins

PARTS OF SPEECH: Verbs

Determine if the tense is present, past, or future. Write none if the tense is not present, past, or future.

4. A. Mary **walked** home.
   B. Carry **has** just **sat** there.
   C. **Will** you **measure** this?
   D. A lady **runs** that firm.

SENTENCE COMBINING:

5. The Lart family transferred.
   Mrs. Lart works for an electronics company.
   The company moved Mrs. Lart and her family from Ohio to Texas.

CAPITALIZATION:

1. a polynesian luau was hosted by the yang family.

PUNCTUATION:

2. Chanda said Maria and Kesi my cousins cant visit on Friday June 12

PARTS OF SPEECH: Verbs

3. Which two tenses will **never** have auxiliary (helping) verbs?

DIRECT OBJECTS/INDIRECT OBJECTS:

   Select the direct object(s) and indirect object(s).

4. Nikko has given Dad and me some tools.

SENTENCE COMBINING:

5. A new typewriter was purchased.
   The new typewriter is self-correcting.
   The new typewriter was placed in our classroom.

Day 138

CAPITALIZATION:

1. at the daisy food company, one can buy polish sausage and lasco* crackers.
*brand name

PUNCTUATION:

2. Ms Jones our ex teacher now works for Gat Co 52 Elm St

PARTS OF SPEECH: Adjectives
Select any adjectives.

3. Our older sister received those large plaques for outstanding achievement.

PARTS OF SPEECH: Prepositions and Adverbs
Determine if the boldfaced word is used as an adverb or a preposition.

4. A. I ran **up** the stairs.
   B. Looking **up**, we saw a jet.

SENTENCE COMBINING:

5. A slowworm is a European lizard.
   It has a smooth, snakelike body.
   It is two to three feet long.

CAPITALIZATION:

1.   45 trow street
                                      salem, oregon
                                      july 9

   dear little ann,

PUNCTUATION:

2. Mrs Dil may I have the following a comb a scarf and a pin

PARTS OF SPEECH: Adverbs

3. Write the comparative form of **well**.

PARTS OF SPEECH: Pronouns
      Select the correct pronoun.

4. May John and _____ (I, me) take that?

SENTENCE COMBINING:

5. The rolls were soft and chewy.
   They had just been taken from the oven.
   The rolls were brushed with melted butter.

Day 140

CAPITALIZATION:

1. the book, <u>autobiography of my mother,</u> will be published by glone enterprises.

PUNCTUATION:

2. The forts gate is closed but will open at 830 A M said the guard

SUBJECTS/VERBS:

Underline the subject once and the verb/verb phrase twice.

3. Martha's father will be good at that.

PARTS OF SPEECH: Adverbs

4. Write the superlative form of **calmly**.

SENTENCE COMBINING:

5. The lady dropped hair dye on her new tile.
It created a permanent stain.
The lady shrieked in frustration.

CAPITALIZATION:

1. the j. o. cone co. celebrates st. patrick's day in an irish restaurant.

PUNCTUATION:

2. Although the clubs name was changed it meets regularly

PARTS OF SPEECH: Adverbs and Prepositions
Determine if the boldfaced word is used as a preposition or an adverb.

3. A. The child ran **around**.
   B. The child ran **around** the room.
   C. The child ran **around** in a circle.

PHRASES/CLAUSES:
Determine if the group of words is a phrase or a clause.

4. A. After we went swimming.
   B. After the game.
   C. Swimming is fun.
   D. Swimming in the lake.

SENTENCE COMBINING:

5. The stream was wide and rocky.
   There was a small waterfall at the end.
   Shallow water spilled over the waterfall.

CAPITALIZATION:

1. during the labor day weekend, our family attended the european fair.

PUNCTUATION:

2. Our team Joe has won the tournament and we are now champions

PARTS OF SPEECH: Adjectives

Write the proper adjective form of the proper noun.

3. A. America
   B. Germany
   C. Indonesia

PARTS OF SPEECH: Adverbs

Select any adverbs.

4. Where are the birds that just flew by?

SENTENCE COMBINING:

5. The plates are small ones.
   They are dirty.
   Dad needs the plates for dinner.
   Someone needs to wash them.

CAPITALIZATION:

Capitalize each title.

1. A. <u>cat on a hot tin roof</u>
   B. <u>i never promised you a rose garden</u>
   C. "rudolph, the red-nosed reindeer"

PUNCTUATION:

2. Wow Ive been elected vice president of our schools council

PARTS OF SPEECH: Verbs

3. List the **23** auxiliary (helping) verbs.

DIRECT OBJECTS: PREDICATE NOMINATIVES

Determine if the word is a direct object or a predicate nominative.

4. A. She licked the **stamp**.
   B. My favorite is that **stamp**.

SENTENCE COMBINING:

5. The teller lost a quarter.
   It rolled behind a chair.
   The customer retrieved it and gave it to the teller.

Day 144

CAPITALIZATION:

1. the republican party met at the dupre hotel in paris.

PUNCTUATION:

2. Casper asked Are you going to Yuma Arizona next week

PARTS OF SPEECH: Pronouns

    Determine if the boldfaced word is a subject, predicate nominative, object of the preposition, direct object, or indirect object.

3. A. Don't go near **them**.
   B. My favorites are Chan and **he**.
   C. Laylah and **I** left.
   D. Maro asked **me** a question.
   E. The dog licked **us**.

PARTS OF SPEECH: Adverbs or Adjectives

    Select the proper form.

4. He talks too _____ (loud, loudly).

SENTENCE COMBINING:

5. Daffodils were potted in red clay pots.
   The daffodils were a brilliant yellow.
   The daffodils were on sale for Mother's Day.

CAPITALIZATION:

1. the chicago museum of art has a picasso painting.

PUNCTUATION:

2.   21 Roe Blvd
                                   Boise Idaho
                                   Sept 21 2006

    Dear Sue

        Weve so much to discuss When youre here well talk
    about our plans

                                   Love
                                   Kathy

LETTER PARTS:
        Review #2 and label the parts.

3.   A.

    B.

        C.

                                D.
                                E.

PARTS OF SPEECH: Verbs
        Select the verb; underline the verb/verb phrase twice.

4. The train must have _____ (went, gone).

SENTENCE COMBINING:

5. The tile was smooth and the color of chocolate.
   The tile was placed on the floor .
   The tile was placed there by two tile-layers.
   They were expert at this.

Day 146

CAPITALIZATION:

1. is pastor lave the minister of that lutheran church on rye road?

PUNCTUATION:

2. Mr Crem frantically took an exam however he passed it

PARTS OF SPEECH: Nouns
Select any abstract nouns.

3. Your honesty and calmness under pressure merit my approval.

PARTS OF SPEECH: Verbs
Select the verb; underline the verb/verb phrase twice.

4. Jan might have _____ (knew, known) the answer.

SENTENCE COMBINING:

5. A tennis ball rolled into the street.
   The child darted after the ball.
   The father yelled at the child to stop.

CAPITALIZATION:

1. during hurricane anne, the waters of the gulf of mexico were turbulent.

PUNCTUATION:

2. Her dad the man in the gray pin striped suit is Prof Hobb

PARTS OF SPEECH: Adverbs and Prepositions
>   Determine if the boldfaced word is an adverb or a preposition.

3. A. The lad crawled **over** the fence.
   B. Come **over**.
   C. I'll come **over** in the morning.

PARTS OF SPEECH: Verbs
>   Determine if the verb is action or linking.

4. A. A walker **became** tired.
   B. Moe **danced** all night.
   C. Her choice **was** a new car.

SENTENCE COMBINING:

5. The group of girls went to the movies.
   The group of boys went to the mall.
   The theater was at the mall.

Day 148

CAPITALIZATION:

1. i like, bev, your photos of the lincoln memorial and the alamo.

PUNCTUATION:

2. The class of 99 held its reunion many attended

PARTS OF SPEECH: Adjectives and Adverbs
        Determine if **good** or **well** should be used in the sentence.

3. A. The lady doesn't feel _____.
    B. You've done a _____ job.
    C. I haven't cleaned _____ today.

PARTS OF SPEECH: Nouns
        Choose the gerund in the sentence.

4. In the summer, swimming is fun.

SENTENCE COMBINING:

5. The old ring was found in the gutter.
    The ring was corroded.
    The ring was a diamond.
    The ring was taken to a jeweler for repair.

CAPITALIZATION:

1. the iberian peninsula consists of the countries of portugal and spain.

PUNCTUATION:

2. Your suggestion as a matter of fact Shawn was an innovative acceptable one

PARTS OF SPEECH: Nouns
    Select nouns.

3. My friend, Bill Cole, is a mechanic for the city of Charleston.

PHRASES/CLAUSES:
    Determine if the group of words is a phrase or a clause.

4. A. If I were you.
   B. Participating in a meeting.
   C. During the long, dry season.

SENTENCE COMBINING:

5. March was cold and rainy
   The wind blew.
   It was our least favorite month.

Day 150

CAPITALIZATION:

1. during the battle of san jacinto, texas won its independence.

PUNCTUATION:
       Punctuate the following titles:

2. A. the chapter, Fossils
    B. the record album, How Great Thou Art
    C. the song, We Are Family

PARTS OF SPEECH: Nouns
       Write the correct possessive form.

3. tips belonging to a waitress

PARTS OF SPEECH: Verbs
       Write the present, past, and past participle.

4. A. to bring
    B. to love
    C. to run

SENTENCE COMBINING:

5. Invitations were purchased for the birthday party.
   Invitations were sent to Paula's friends.
   Paula's friends will meet for a pizza, birthday party.

CAPITALIZATION:

1. does darn paint co. carry peppy girl* paint?

*brand name

PUNCTUATION:

2. His uptight attitude isnt usual and hes usually calm and relaxed

PARTS OF SPEECH: Nouns
    Determine if the boldfaced noun is a subject, predicate nominative, or direct object.

3. A. Jemima tagged the next **swimmer**.
   B. The **swimmer** lost the race.
   C. Dasha is our best **swimmer**.

PARTS OF SPEECH: Verbs

4. Write an example of an **infinitive**.

SENTENCE COMBINING:

5. A podiatrist is a foot doctor.
   Dr. Vargas is my podiatrist.
   He shares a building with Dr. Morgan.
   Dr. Morgan is my aunt.

Day 152

CAPITALIZATION:

Capitalize the following titles:

1. A. "death of a hired man"
   B. the tale of two cities
   C. "the wisdom of life"
   D. "the secret life of walter mitty"

PUNCTUATION:

2. Its a full page picture of Lassie Id like one

PARTS OF SPEECH: Verbs

Write the present, past, and future tense of each infinitive.

3. A. to eat
   B. to freeze
   C. to play

SUBJECTS/VERBS:

Underline the subject once and the verb/verb phrase twice.

4. During the storm, many of the cows wandered into the barn and devoured hay.

SENTENCE COMBINING:

5. The deer walked through the forest.
   He walked to the edge of the field.
   He sniffed the air.
   Then he ambled into the open meadow.

CAPITALIZATION:

1. the andes mountains, running through chile, level at the pacific coast.

PUNCTUATION:
    Punctuate the following:

2. A. the ship, U.S.S. Arizona
    B. a fable, The Fox and the Grapes
    C. a magazine, Toys and Tots

PARTS OF SPEECH: Nouns
    Write the correct possessive form.

3. A. a penny belonging to a child
   B. a horse belonging to two children
   C. a meeting belonging to more than one lady

PARTS OF SPEECH: Pronouns
    Select the correct pronoun.

4. Give _____ (I, me) that.

SENTENCE COMBINING:

5. The student's answer was silly.
   She laughed as she said it.
   The teacher did not laugh.
   The teacher frowned and reprimanded her.

Day 154

CAPITALIZATION:

1. a new mall, darway village, is located east of keen drive.

PUNCTUATION:

2. The boys tired and disgruntled counted only three fourths of the coupons

TYPES OF SENTENCES:
        Write the sentence type.

3. A. A rose is in the vase.
   B. Ugh! I touched it!
   C. Has he finished?
   D. Please sit down.

PARTS OF SPEECH: Adverbs
        Determine the correct word.

4. Dave never tells us (nothing, anything).

SENTENCE COMBINING:

5. The ice cream bar was chocolate.
   It was purchased from a street vendor.
   The hot sun made it melt quickly.

Day 155

CAPITALIZATION:

1. in greek literature we studied goddesses like venus in mythology.

PUNCTUATION:

2. Remove the extra p in papper and its correct Fred

PARTS OF SPEECH: Adverbs

3. I can't do (anything, nothing).

FRAGMENTS/SENTENCES/RUN-ONS:

Determine if each group of words is a fragment, a sentence, or a run-on.

4. A. Pat waited patiently.
   B. The dog growled, it then ran away.
   C. The one in the middle.

SENTENCE COMBINING:

5. The sprinkling system was placed in our yard.
   Grandpa and Dad dug the trench.
   Mom and Grandma laid the pipe.

Day 156

CAPITALIZATION:

1. the new york philharmonic orchestra might perform at carnegie hall.

PUNCTUATION:

2. Tom we need hay horses and a wagon for the hayride said Cass

PARTS OF SPEECH: Pronouns
        Choose the possessive pronoun that agrees with the antecedent.

3. Be sure that each has (her, their) items.

PARTS OF SPEECH: Adjectives
        Select any adjectives.

4. An oak tree grew in the empty lot for twenty years.

SENTENCE COMBINING:

5. The cow chewed its cud.
   The cow meandered across the field.
   Flies swarmed around the cow.

CAPITALIZATION:

1. the roman catholic church celebrated a christmas mass.

PUNCTUATION:

2. The Poe Co gave its honored retiring employee a round trip ticket to China

PARTS OF SPEECH: Nouns
   Write the plural form.

3. A. octopus
   B. crash
   C. payment
   D. cry
   E. birthday

BUSINESS LETTERS:

4. Use your own address for the heading and the following information. You are writing a business letter to Mar Co., 4 West Org St., Detroit, MI. Set up the heading, the inside address, and the salutation.

SENTENCE COMBINING:

5. Jan's younger brother invested in the stock market.
   He's made money.
   Jan's other brother invested in the stock market.
   He's lost money.

Day 158

CAPITALIZATION:

1. are the villa nova apartments two blocks south of carp mountain?

PUNCTUATION:

2. Your bank by the way was closed for Washingtons Birthday remarked Jay

PARTS OF SPEECH: Nouns
   Select any nouns.

3. A plane crashed into a mountain and caused a major avalanche.

CLAUSES:
   Determine if the group of words is a **dependent** or an **independent** clause.

4. A. Today is great!
    B. If you must wish.
    C. Although we might be invited to the wedding.

SENTENCE COMBINING:

5. The check was sent through the mail.
   The check was for twenty dollars.
   The check was sent from Harry Tye.
   The check was payment for a book.

CAPITALIZATION:

1. the brim dog company sells french poodles and brittany spaniels.

PUNCTUATION:

2. Yipee We girls scored twenty two points at last nights game

PARTS OF SPEECH: Pronouns
   Select the correct pronoun.

3. The first one to leave was _____ (me, I).

PARTS OF SPEECH: Adverbs
   Select any adverbs.

4. Together, we shall not have to work so hard.

SENTENCE COMBINING:

5. Sally worked her way through college.
   Sally worked as a waitress.
   Sally graduated from college last May.

Day 160

CAPITALIZATION:

1. a new mexico flag was beside "old glory"* in a recent veteran's day parade.

   *a nickname

PUNCTUATION:

2. His down trodden view cant help Steves problem

FRAGMENTS:
   Determine if the group of words is a fragment.

3. A. Talking to my mother.
   B. Frank in the afternoon.
   C. The team drills often.

PARTS OF SPEECH: Preposition or Adverb
   Determine if the boldfaced word is a preposition or an adverb.

4. A. Kim played **outside** for an hour.
   B. Kim played **outside**.
   C. Kim sat **outside** the door.

SENTENCE COMBINING:

5. The townhouse was spacious.
   It had two fireplaces.
   It had a skylight.
   The couple purchased it.

CAPITALIZATION:

1. the louisiana territory was explored by lewis, clark, and a shoshone indian, sacajawea.

PUNCTUATION:

2. Your well written paper however has too many thes

PHRASES/CLAUSES:

Determine if the group of words is a phrase or a clause.

3. A. After the game.
   B. After they left.

PARTS OF SPEECH: Adverbs

Select adverbs.

4. We can't proceed further now.

SENTENCE COMBINING:

5. We played cards.
   Before that, we went to a movie.
   After the card game, we read.

Day 162

CAPITALIZATION:

1. in the spring, some leukemia patients visited a cape cod hospital in new england.

PUNCTUATION:

2. Beths article Lifes Benefits appeared on the thirty second page of the magazine Bronze

SUBJECTS/VERBS:

Underline the subject once and the verb/verb phrase twice.

3. During a period of reflection, some of the women were praying.

PARTS OF SPEECH: Adjectives

Select adjectives.

4. An American rose bush grew in a shaded area.

SENTENCE COMBINING:

5. The artist set up his easel.
   The paints were assembled.
   The artist accidentally knocked over his easel and paints.

CAPITALIZATION:

1. in biology I, ms. gore explained mendell's theory of heredity.

PUNCTUATION:

2. Susans father Im told is an author a professor and a director

PARTS OF SPEECH: Verbs
        Select the correct verb; underline the verb phrase twice.

3. Priscilla should have _____ (risen, raised) the flag.

PARTS OF SPEECH: Pronouns
        Select the correct pronoun.

4. Is the winner _____ (he, him)?

SENTENCE COMBINING:

5. Dr. Hill wrote a prescription.
   The prescription was for penicillin.
   Dr. Hill asked the patient if she were allergic to penicillin.

Day 164

CAPITALIZATION:

1. the gulf of taranto is an arm of the mediterranean sea founded by the greeks in the eighth century.

PUNCTUATION:

2. Kens family will arrive at 8 A M for the St Jerome wedding said the writer

PARTS OF SPEECH: Adjectives or Adverbs
　　　Select the correct answer.

3. Your voice seems (softer, more softly) than mine.

PARTS OF SPEECH: Verbs
　　　Select the correct verb.

4. The baby had _____ (laid, lain) quietly for ten minutes.

SENTENCE COMBINING:

5. The card was a birthday one.
　It had roses on the front.
　It had a poem inside.
　It was sent by Cal to his mom.

CAPITALIZATION:

1. the english soccer team played at longson park near piccadilly square.

PUNCTUATION:

2. Joes essay has too many ands therefore it scored a 3

PARTS OF SPEECH: Conjunctions

3. Give the three most common coordinating conjunctions.

PARTS OF SPEECH: Nouns

    Select nouns.

4. During the charity ball, his donation reflected his amazing generosity.

SENTENCE COMBINING:

5. The bird drank water.
   The bird was a robin.
   The bird drank from a bird bath.
   The bird drank and flew to a nearby branch.

Day 166

CAPITALIZATION:

1. "this day," replied nan, "is the beginning of mardi gras."

PUNCTUATION:

2. On Oct 23 1991 her daughter was born in Baltimore Md

PARTS OF SPEECH: Verbs
     Write the present, past, and past participle form.

3. A. to break
   B. to show
   C. to lie (rest)
   D. to yell

FRAGMENTS/SENTENCES/RUN-ONS:
     Determine if the group of words is a fragment, sentence, or run-on.

4. A. If you go, take me.
   B. He is ill, he'll have to leave.
   C. I this with you.

SENTENCE COMBINING:

5. Ron has a wagon.
   It's red.
   It's large.
   He received it as a gift from his uncle.
   Ron doesn't play with his wagon.

CAPITALIZATION:

1. when tracey had mumps, she played chinese checkers and read the book, <u>the diary of anne frank</u>.

PUNCTUATION:

2. Yes well go to Montezumas Castle my friend

PARTS OF SPEECH: Nouns
      Select the predicate nominative.

3. The best person for the job was Mr. Dobbs.

PHRASES/CLAUSES:
      Determine if the group of words is a phrase or a clause.

4. A. Down the street.
   B. Walking down the street.
   C. When you are walking down the street.
   D. I'll walk with you down the street.

SENTENCE COMBINING:

5. The clothes were stacked in a pile.
   The clothes were dirty.
   The clothes belonged to Christy.
   Christy refused to do her laundry.
   Now her mom refuses to do Christy's laundry.

Day 168

CAPITALIZATION:

1. our address, lisa, is 24 fob lane, st. louis, missouri.

PUNCTUATION:

2. Carl is going to the states boundary but Im going to Hartford Conn

PARTS OF SPEECH: Pronouns

      Determine the antecedent of the possessive.

3. The wolf lost **its** way.

PARTS OF SPEECH: Conjunctions

4. Write examples of correlative conjunctions.

SENTENCE COMBINING:

5. The cricket crawled along the kitchen floor of the new home.
   It was the first cricket the family had seen.
   The family knew that this was a sign that there would be more.

CAPITALIZATION:

1. did gov. litton speak to the kiwanis club about american intervention in cuban affairs?

PUNCTUATION:

2. The U S S Arizona a ship at Pearl Harbor Hawaii was a victim of Japans attack

PARTS OF SPEECH: Adverbs
        Select adverbs.

3. Afterward the team didn't go anywhere to celebrate.

PARTS OF SPEECH: Pronouns

4. List the objective pronouns.

SENTENCE COMBINING:

5. Has anyone seen Mike's checkbook?
    It's blue and leather.
    It's for Banter Bank.
    Mike is searching desperately for it.

CAPITALIZATION:

1. the poem entitled "to my wife" begins, "i love sharing...," and appears in an american anthology.

PUNCTUATION:

2. His father in law James Brooks is Sen J J Brooks said Faye

PARTS OF SPEECH: Pronouns
   Select the correct pronoun.

3. To _____ (who, whom) did you give this test?

PARTS OF SPEECH: Adverbs and Prepositions
   Determine if the boldfaced word is an adverb or a preposition.

4. A. Did you crawl **under** the bridge?
   B. He looked **under** but couldn't find it.

SENTENCE COMBINING:

5. One of the books was lost.
   The librarian was upset.
   A student returned the lost book.
   The librarian was pleased.

CAPITALIZATION:

1. the dancers from royal dance academy presented a ballet at singe nursing home in cheyenne.

PUNCTUATION:

2. Well give you said Edna the up to date records of that camp

PARTS OF SPEECH: Adjectives

    Select adjectives.

3. Fresh, hot, onion rings were served in several small wicker baskets.

PARTS OF SPEECH:

4. Write an example of a **reflexive pronoun**.

SENTENCE COMBINING:

5. The children walked a mile to school.
   The children walked down a lane.
   The lane was deserted.
   The school bus picked them up at the end of the lane.

Day 172

CAPITALIZATION:

1. in the <u>new testament's</u> book of <u>matthew,</u> you can read about early christians.

PUNCTUATION:

2. This months Bread and Bran magazine contains these recipes muffins raisin breads and pancakes

SUBJECTS/VERBS:

       Select the correct verb.

3. A. Either Mary or the boys (lives, live) in town.
   B. Either the boys or Mary (lives, live) in town.

FRAGMENTS/SENTENCES/RUN-ONS:

       Determine if the group of words is a fragment, sentence, or run-on.

4. A. The nut bread too soggy.
   B. Go!
   C. Jim's not going he's ill.

SENTENCE COMBINING:

5. The night was starry.
   The couple ate a late dinner.
   They ate at an outside cafe.
   They browsed in several art galleries.
   They were celebrating their anniversary.

CAPITALIZATION:

1. the hellenistic age lasted until rome took control of lands that border much of the mediterranean sea.

PUNCTUATION:

2. If youre going to the Lakers game dont wear your two tone jeans

PARTS OF SPEECH: Nouns

3. Write an example of an appositive.

PARTS OF SPEECH: Adjectives
   Select the correct adjective.

4. Of the two, this mattress is (softer, softest).

SENTENCE COMBINING:

5. Her parents went to Europe.
   They landed in London.
   They ferried across the English Channel.
   They took a train through France, Spain, and Portugal.

Day 174

CAPITALIZATION:

1. the crusades were fought between muslim turks and christians.

PUNCTUATION:

2. Kimis favorite magazine Photography Today has an article about cameras

SENTENCE TYPES:

Write the type of sentence.

3. A. Snow fell.
   B. Is snow falling?
   C. Snow fell today!
   D. Shake the snow from your boots.

ENVELOPES:

4. Address an envelope. Use your home address. Send it to Monti Banks, 34 Drift Street, Day Creek, Oregon   97429.

SENTENCE COMBINING:

5. The library opens at ten.
   There is a story hour at noon.
   The library is also having a stress seminar at 7 P.M.

CAPITALIZATION:

1. has mary read <u>how to eat fried worms</u> at horne public library?

PUNCTUATION:

2. Cant you make the ts on the sign larger asked Barry

PARTS OF SPEECH:

3. Write 10 linking verbs.

PARTS OF SPEECH: Adjectives

      Select adjectives.

4. Her funny, witty father wrote that very hilarious story.

SENTENCE COMBINING:

5. The letters were sent to the governor.
    The letters concerned the freeway proposal.
    The governor sent a letter in reply.

CAPITALIZATION:

1. the member of the orlando reading council met with mayor cortez at the patina hotel.

PUNCTUATION:

2. Although everyones choice was water skiing Id rather go fishing

PARTS OF SPEECH: Nouns
>   Write the plural.

3. A. party
    B. ceiling
    C. elk
    D. patience

PARTS OF SPEECH: Pronouns
>   Select the correct possessive pronoun.

4. Someone left (their, his) books.

SENTENCE COMBINING:

5. Bedtime is eight o'clock for the little ones.
    They must take a bath and put on pajamas at seven o'clock.
    Someone reads them a book.

CAPITALIZATION:

1. after the bolshevik revolution, the communist party took over russia.

PUNCTUATION:

2. Her idea the one about self inflating balloons caught an inventors attention

PARTS OF SPEECH: Pronouns
    Select the antecedent for the boldfaced possessive.

3. During the morning, the mother took **her** children to school.

SUBJECTS/VERBS:
    Underline the subject once and verb/verb phrase twice.

4. Around the corner from his home is a bank with a special computer.

SENTENCE COMBINING:

5. The chair was broken.
   Dad repaired it.
   It broke again.
   Dad threw it away.

Day 178

CAPITALIZATION:

1. in the eastern region of lancaster county, many pennsylvania dutch and amish people live.

PUNCTUATION:

2. Susan her voice soft replied Youre the exconvict whos now our missions leader

SUBJECTS/VERBS:
    Underline the subject once and verb/verb phrase twice.

3. Cabot and his group of men sailed to America and claimed it for England.

PARTS OF SPEECH: Pronouns
    Select the correct pronoun.

4. Either the girls or _____ (I, me) will go.

SENTENCE COMBINING:

5. There were two plants in the brass container.
   One was a living ficus, and one was a silk.
   The living one is shedding its leaves.

CAPITALIZATION:

1. our spanish history class planted a mexican fan palm in honor of cinco de mayo*.

   *special holiday

PUNCTUATION:
   Use underlining or quotation marks.

2. A. the play, Ivan
   B. the book, Playful Poetry
   C. the movie, Conrad
   D. the magazine, Hair Ideas

PARTS OF SPEECH: Verbs
   Select the past participle form; underline the verb phrase twice.

3. Could Jasper have _____ (went, gone) earlier?

BUSINESS LETTERS:

4. Write an example of an inside address.

SENTENCE COMBINING:

5. The van had a cracked windshield.
   The van had a dent in its back door.
   The van was only two years old.
   The van had been involved in a recent accident.

Day 180

CAPITALIZATION:

1. last spring we boarded a trans european jet and flew over tengri khan, the highest mountain of the tien shan mountains of southeastern asia.

PUNCTUATION:

2. Morisas dad the self reliant leader is here youll want to meet him

PARTS OF SPEECH: Verbs
Select the verb.

3. Has Nam _____ (laid, lain) the equipment there?

FRAGMENTS/SENTENCES/RUN-ONS:
Determine if the group of words is a fragment, sentence, or run-on.

4. A. A rabbit in the garden all night.
   B. We walked and talked for over an hour.
   C. The time has come I must leave.
   D. Having planted a garden.
   E. After you take out the garbage.

SENTENCE COMBINING:

5. To make that dessert, add boiling water to the package mixture.
   Add ice water.
   Stir until dissolved.
   Then, chill.

DAILY GRAMS ANSWER KEY:

AMV/RA: = ANSWERS MAY VARY/REPRESENTATIVE ANSWERS

DAY 1: 1. My, Mesa, High, School 2. The answer, in fact, is in the book. 3. noun (abstract noun) 4. drunk; <u>has drunk</u> 5. AMV/RA: The angry boy threw the eraser at his sister. Angrily, the boy threw an eraser at his sister. Because he was angry, the boy threw an eraser at his sister.

DAY 2: 1. Last, Yellowstone, National, Park 2. Mary, have you seen my binoculars? 3. The, beautiful, white, a, peaceful 4. A. children B. moose C. oxen 5. AMV/RA: The lost, crying child was looking for her mother. The lost child was crying and looking for her mother.

DAY 3: 1. We, Judge, Barnworth, Kiwanis, Club 2. Jill exclaimed, "Give me the ticket!" 3. milk 4. abstract noun 5. AMV/RA: The puppet show would soon begin; therefore, everyone crowded quickly into the auditorium. Because the puppet show would soon begin, everyone crowded quickly into the auditorium.

DAY 4: 1. Did, Napoleon, Battle, Waterloo 2. The correct route to take, I believe, is Route 42. 3. A. imperative (command) B. declarative (statement)** 4. infinitive 5. AMV/RA: The black homeless horse roamed the countryside. The horse, black and homeless, roamed the countryside.

Students need to learn **sentence types; eventually a selection of types will not be given.

DAY 5: 1. The, Success, Through, Positive, Mental, Attitude 2. That address should be 500 Willow Lane, Atlanta, Georgia. 3. <u>s</u> (classes), <u>x</u> (boxes), <u>z</u> (buzzes), <u>sh</u> (wishes), and <u>ch</u> (churches)*** 4. now, later 5. AMV/RA: An emerald and diamond ring was lost; it was valued at ten thousand dollars. An emerald and diamond ring, valued at ten thousand dollars, was lost.

***This rule needs to be learned; it will appear throughout this text.

DAY 6: 1. The, Red, Cross, Association, Friday, Governor, Jonas, T., Phelps 2. "I want a milkshake," said Tony. 3. direct object = race 4. <u>owner</u> and <u>company</u> <u>have agreed</u> 5.
AMV/RA: During the rain, the car was stalled in the middle of the intersection. In the middle of the intersection, the stalled car sputtered in the rain.****

****A comma is used after two introductory, prepositional phrases.

DAY 7: 1. Should, I, Grandma, Rustlers', Restaurant 2. My family and I went to Bangor, Maine, last summer. 3. run; <u>has run</u> 4. <u>Tom</u> or <u>brother</u> <u>will be going</u> 5. AMV/RA: Lori's mother, who is a member of the church choir, sang a solo last Sunday. Lori's mother, a member of the church choir, sang a solo last Sunday.

DAY 8: 1. Washington, D., C., East (region) 2. Because school wasn't open, John went to the mall. 3. (You) (you understood) <u>give</u> 4. A. interrogative B. exclamatory 5. AMV/RA: Dr. Marlowe, our veterinarian, has given our dog a shot for a leg infection. Because our dog's leg was infected, Dr. Marlowe, our veterinarian, has given her a shot.

DAY 9: 1. The, Papago, Indian, Reservation, Arizona, (not eastern, a direction) 2. Harry's birthday is Feb. 28, 1987. 3. A. action (direct object = artichoke) B. linking (<u>milk</u> <u>tastes</u> sour) 4. Air is a concrete noun. (Although air is invisible to the naked eye, the molecules can be seen with specialized equipment.) 5. AMV/RA: Laughing children made sand castles as they played in the sand. Playing in the sand, the children laughed and made sand castles.

DAY 10: 1. An, Alaskan, Aleutian, Islands 2. On Saturday, March 7, 1927, they were married. 3. A. action (direct object = way) B. linking 4. A. bugs B. mice C. deer D. watches 5. AMV/RA: The policewoman stopped the speeding driver and gave him* a ticket. A speeding driver was given a ticket by a policewoman.
   *or her

DAY 11: 1. Has, Fanny's, Fudge, Factory, Brookside, Drive 2. Tom Sweeny, the store manager, will give you a refund, Susan. 3. <u>One</u> <u>left</u> and <u>returned</u> 4. Ominous, black, the, bright 5. AMV/RA: Jill, an only child who is spoiled, is allowed to do what she wishes. Jill is allowed to do that which she wishes because she is a spoiled, only child.

DAY 12: 1. My, Aunt, Tara, Carmichael, Romero's, Drugstore 2. Although Kami won't visit, she'll send cards. 3. warm 4. There are 23 helping verbs: is, am, are, was, were, be, being, been, has, have, had, do, does, did, may, might, must, can, could, will, would, shall, should 5. AMV/RA: The broken, antique vase lay in small pieces on the floor. Smashed into small bits, the antique vase lay broken on the floor.

DAY 13: 1. Have, Kansas, State, Fair, Wendy 2. Your reading test will be tomorrow; be sure to study.
    Note to teacher: You may want to accept this written as two sentences. "Your reading test will be tomorrow. Be sure to study."

3. stolen; <u>had been stolen</u> 4. I 5. AMV/RA: The chocolate milk soured because Tom left it out. Because Tom left the chocolate milk out, it soured.

DAY 14: 1. In, The, Tale, Two, Cities 2. No, you're not to blame; it isn't anyone's fault. 3. ~~During the storm~~ several trees fell ~~by the side of the road~~. 4. AMV/RA: A. Mississippi River B. George Washington C. Thunderbird Bank D. Pioneer School 5. AMV/RA: Jill wanted to eat breakfast in a cafeteria, not in a restaurant. Not wanting to eat at the restaurant, Jill suggested a cafeteria.

DAY 15: 1. The, French, Uptown, Grooming, Shoppe, Saturday 2. Joe's dad, a lawyer, flew to Omaha, Nebraska, today. 3. hair, salon 4. is, am, are, was, were, be, being, been, do, does, did, has, have, had, may, must, might, will, would, shall, should, can, could 5. AMV/RA: The Oriental chef cut the vegetables and fried the fish as he cooked at our table. Cooking at our table, the Oriental chef cut vegetables and fried fish.

DAY 16: 1. Do, Mr., Mrs., Colena, Baptist, Iowa 2. We purchased French fries, a shake, and a hamburger, Vince. 3. and, but, or 4. <u>sister</u> <u>changed</u>, <u>works</u> 5. AMV/RA: The digital clock that had been given to my father as a gift was broken. The broken digital clock had been given to my father as a gift.

DAY 17: 1. Has, German 2. Do you, Marsha, have a sketch for the children's playground? 3. clause 4. interjection 5. AMV/RA: The potted tulip, a gift from Grandma to Mom, is dying. Grandma gave the potted tulip to Mom as a gift; unfortunately, it's dying.

DAY 18: 1. Was, Century, Elementary, School, Valentine's, Day 2. I. Birds / A. Types / 1. Migrating / 2. Non-migrating / B. Habitats 3. Yesterday, sooner 4. drunk; should have drunk (*Not* is an adverb.) 5. AMV/RA: Although Jim planted flowers in the garden, he forgot to water them. Jim planted flowers in the garden, but he forgot to water them.*

*In the last sentence, be sure that students understand a comma is required because two complete sentences are joined.

DAY 19: 1. Last, Swiss 2. This rug, most certainly, was made in China. 3. swims 4. Letters, bills, and stamps were lying 5. AMV/RA: The wildlife book, open to a chapter about moose, was lying on the table. The wildlife book, which was open to a chapter about moose, was lying on the table.
   Note: One could argue about restrictive and non-restrictive clauses. Commas have been used here.

DAY 20: 1. Each, Smith, Pasadena, Tournament, Roses, Parade, California 2. Did Mary, the junior cheerleader, go with you? 3. clause (rain slackened) This is a dependent clause because it cannot stand alone as a complete thought. 4. work 5. AMV/RA: A delicious lunch of soup and sandwiches was served at noon. For lunch at noon, soup and sandwiches were served.

DAY 21: 1. Some, Dutch, Metrocenter, Mall, Phoenix 2. "What," she asked, "is the answer to the problem?" 3. paper 4. was (*One* is the subject; cross out the prepositional phrase *of the children*.) 5. AMV/RA: Mr. Samuels repaired the typewriter; the charge for repair was $9.00. When Mr. Samuels repaired the typewriter, the cost was $9.00.

DAY 22: 1. At, Christmas, Kennedy, Airport, New, York 2. No, your answer, to say the least, wasn't wrong. 3. is, am, are, was, were, be, being, been, has, have, had, do, does, did, shall, should, will, would, can, could, may, must, might 4. center, learning, June 5. AMV/RA: Dropping the fork as he served the salad, the waiter became embarrassed. The salad was served by an embarrassed waiter who had dropped a fork.

DAY 23: 1. My, Uncle, Jim, Potomac, River, Department, Education 2. Your t's need to be crossed, but the other letters are fine. 3. needs (Each needs) 4. C. imperative 5. AMV/RA: When my sister put green flowered wallpaper in her kitchen, it fell off. The green flowered wallpaper that my sister put in her kitchen fell off.

DAY 24: 1. During, Easter, Sell's, Nursing, Home, West, Palm, Lane 2. 22 East Dow / Gettysburg, PA 17325 / January 21, 2004 / Dear Mrs. Parks, 3. heading / salutation or greeting 4. come; should have come 5. AMV/RA: The floor, sticky with honey, needs to be washed. Because the floor is sticky with honey, it needs to be washed.

DAY 25: 1. Are, Great, Plains, Midwest 2. Giant black ants emerged from the ground and marched across the lawn. 3. will stay/shall stay 4. AMV/RA: The horse was running down the street. Running down the street, I lost a shoe. 5. AMV/RA: The yard was filled with mud; however, Joe went out to play. Although the yard was filled with mud, Joe went to play.

DAY 26: 1. The, St., James, Lutheran, Church, Columbus, Day 2. If Lieut. Jones can't join us, let's go to a show. 3. jar, top, refrigerator 4. (You) give (This is an imperative sentence with *you understood* as a subject.) 5. AMV/RA: A beautician cut her client's long hair into a short bob. The client's once-long hair was cut into a bob by a beautician.

DAY 27: 1. The, <u>Bible</u>, Spanish, Mexico 2. I need the following: eggs, milk, and bread. 3. ribbon 4. player 5. AMV/RA: Jane had a good time skiing with her family at Vail. Skiing at Vail with her family, Jane had a good time.

DAY 28: 1. Did, Hiawatha, Iroquois, Indian, East 2. The streets were flooded; therefore, only large trucks used it. 3. more energetic 4. A. monkeys B. brooks C. octopi/octopuses D. secretaries E. geese 5. AMV/RA: Because the heel of Jeanie's shoe was broken, she threw the shoe away. The heel of Jeanie's shoe was broken; therefore, she threw the shoe away.

DAY 29: 1. We, Franco's, Begay's, Grocery 2. "Use a three-pronged fork to pitch the hay," said the farmer. 3. <u>principal/teachers</u> <u>could attend</u> 4. too, very 5. AMV/RA: Happy children watched eagerly as the dolphins performed. The children, happy and eager, watched as the dolphins performed.

DAY 30: 1. The, Museum, Natural, History, Arctic 2. The story entitled "All summer in a Day" is in the book, <u>Thrust</u>. 3. <u>neighbors</u> <u>had introduced</u> 4. I (A simple explanation is that the sentence could read, **"Martha runs faster than I run."** *Run* has been deleted.) 5. AMV/RA: The girls went to the library and then ice skated for two hours. After the girls went to the library, they ice skated for two hours.

DAY 31: 1. The, England, Atlantic, Ocean, North, Sea 2. We cleaned the house, and Mom gave the car a tune-up. 3. book, pictures, spaceship 4. A. heading B. greeting or salutation C. body D. closing E. signature 5. AMV/RA: Despite the forecast of rain, a picnic was planned. Although the weather is sunny for our picnic, the forecast is for rain.

DAY 32: 1. The, <u>U.S.S.</u>, <u>Constitution</u>, <u>All</u>, <u>About</u>, <u>History</u> 2. On Feb. 14, 1912, Arizona was admitted to the Union. 3. clause (<u>time was changed</u>) 4. Determinedly, hard 5. AMV/RA: The owners were pleased with the professional paint job. The painting of the house, done by professionals, pleased the owners.

DAY 33: 1. When, Brian, Oak, Junior, College, Dr., Coe's, Calculus 2. Joe retorted, "Are you, by the way, leaving? I'd like a ride." 3. his (antecedent = Everybody) 4. <u>one Is</u> <u>entertaining</u> 5. AMV/RA: The story, "The Cask of Amontillado," is in both our English and reading books. Not only is "The Cask of Amontillado" in our English book, but also it's in our reading text.

DAY 34: 1. The, The, Last, Mohicans, Brack's Theater 2. The book, <u>Mother Goose's Tales</u>,* contained the nursery rhyme entitled "Hickory Dickory Dock."
    *Some teach that no commas are required.
 3. laid (direct object = tile) 4. A. (has, have, had) thrown B. (has, have, had) sworn C. (has, have, had) lain D. (has, have, had) given E. (has, have, had) burst 5. AMV/RA: Because it's spring, the dogwood tree is blooming. The dogwood tree blooms in the spring.

DAY 35: 1. The, My, Life, Has, Changed, I 2. Twenty-one of the eighty-four, or one-fourth, was the answer. 3. That, new, dirty 4. will speak/shall speak 5. AMV/RA: The purpose of the free Utah pamphlets is to encourage tourism. The pamphlets to encourage tourism in Utah are free.

DAY 36: 1. If, Sharon, American, American, Revolution, Boston, Massacre 2. Ms. Simms said, "Please come to my office." 3. blue 4. declarative 5. AMV/RA: The McGrew painting in the living room is crooked. The McGrew painting, the one hanging in the living room, is crooked.

DAY 37: 1. The, The, Testing, Intelligence 2. Tom Sellers, D.D.S., is offering free, dental check-ups. 3. clause (<u>fish were biting</u>) 4. steadily, fast 5. AMV/RA: The vegetables, beans and carrots, that were planted in May are growing nicely. The beans and carrots planted in May are growing nicely.

DAY 38: 1. During, Ice, Age, Atlantic, Ocean 2. If you leave early, lock the door, Mary. 3. swum; <u>have swum</u> 4. <u>Some</u> <u>had flown</u> (Note: Geese cannot be the subject; geese is the object of the preposition.) 5. AMV/RA: Theo helped the elderly lady whose purse contents were scattered on the ground and sidewalk. The elderly lady's purse contents were scattered on the sidewalk; Theo helped retrieve the contents.

DAY 39: 1. Does, Dr., Partin, Jefferson, Medical, Building 2. On Mon., Dec. 21, 1986, the A.M.A. met in St. Paul, Minn. 3. infinitive 4. she (The sentence might read, **"Mary speaks more clearly than she does."**) 5. AMV/RA: Someone yelled at him; hence, his feelings are hurt, and he won't talk. When someone yelled at him, his feelings were hurt, and he wouldn't talk.

DAY 40: 1. Have, Captain, Jones, Mayor, Flood, Sears, Tower, Chicago 2. Does John's essay contain too many <u>but's</u>? 3. middle (in the middle), dinner (of dinner), store (to the store) 4. There are several ways of correcting this run-on: A. We'll go to the beach; Jane will drive us. B. We'll go to the beach since Jane will drive us. C. We'll go to the beach, and Jane will drive us. D. We'll go to the beach. Jane will drive us. 5. AMV/RA: Uncle Jim, a lawyer with an office downtown, has Susie's dad for a client. Uncle Jim, whose office is downtown, has Susie's dad for a client.

DAY 41: 1. In, India, Hindu 2. Because it's raining, we will stay indoors. 3. A. past B. future C. present 4. home, back, out 5. AMV/RA: That man, a custodian at Grant School, is my grandfather. My grandfather is the custodian who works at Grant School.

DAY 42: 1. Last, Harrington (***Chicken pox*** is a disease and isn't capitalized.) 2. Jill, have you seen my dog, the black and shaggy one? 3. A. wherries B. bays C. neighbors D. glasses 4. ~~Throughout the day~~, the <u>ranchers</u> <u>had driven</u> ~~in their trucks~~. 5. AMV/RA: During John's first attempt at making cookies, he stirred brown sugar into the batter. John, making cookies for the first time, stirred brown sugar into the batter.

DAY 43: 1. Ben, Franklin, Constitutional, Convention, Philadelphia 2. Although the ladies' club met, no decision was made. 3. dog 4. rocker (<u>item</u> = rocker) 5. AMV/RA: The red and green pens on the art table are being used to make Christmas decorations. On the art table are red and green pens that are being used for making Christmas decorations.

DAY 44: 1. Does, Jean, Governor, Brown 2. Dear Miss Lyons, / Yes, I'd love to visit you.(!) / Sincerely, / Ted 3. A. adjective (some popcorn) B. pronoun 4. conjunctions 5. AMV/RA: The cast iron pan on the stove is greasy from frying bacon. The greasy, cast iron pan on the stove was used to fry bacon.

DAY 45: 1. Our, Vice-President, United, States, Senate 2. The first song in the book, <u>Worship Him</u>, is entitled "We Have Come into This House." 3. <u>One</u> ~~of the children~~ <u>is playing</u> ~~with wooden blocks~~. 4. is (<u>group is</u>) 5. AMV/RA: Our two-month-old television is broken; the repair person will come today. Because our new television is broken, a repair person will come today.

DAY 46: 1. The, Sunset, Point, Phoenix, Camp, Verde 2. Yes, if I am correct, the answer is fifty-five. 3. A. preposition (prepositional phrase = *up the chimney*) B. adverb (**Up** tells where we looked.) 4. interjection 5. AMV/RA: The Siamese cat purrs softly when stroked. The cat, a Siamese, purrs softly when stroked.

DAY 47: 1. Have, He, Shall, Cover, Me, Feathers 2. In Laguna Beach, California, there are many beautiful, hillside homes. 3. A. concrete B. abstract C. abstract D. concrete (**Air** is concrete because it can be separated into molecules.) 4. broken; <u>must have broken</u> 5. AMV/RA: Abby, our school's champion tennis player, will participate in a state tournament. Abby, who will participate in a state tournament, is our school's champion tennis player.

DAY 48: 1. The, Democratic, Party, Dad, Miami 2. The <u>Queen Mary</u> is in the harbor at Long Beach, California. 3. imperative 4. A. present B. future C. past 5. AMV/RA: The ten dollar check was cashed by the teller. The check, written for ten dollars, was cashed by the teller.

DAY 49: 1. The, Cape, Good, Hope, Africa 2. The blue three-tiered curtains were discarded. 3. has, have, had, do, does, did, may, might, must, shall, should, will, would, can, could, is, am, are, was, were, be, being, been (Note: Students should memorize and **learn** this list.) 4. A. beautiful B. honest C. practical D. friendly 5. AMV/RA: The closed, Chinese restaurant will reopen in the morning. Although presently closed, the Chinese restaurant will open in the morning.

DAY 50: 1. Our, Bristol, Lake, Mummy, Mountain, Drive 2. Your warranty expires Jan. 2; don't forget.(!) 3. sneaked 4. My, its 5. AMV/RA: The black and white cows in the barn have been milked.

DAY 51: 1. Have, Grand, Central, Station, New, York, City 2. The following are needed for dessert: apples, pie, and cake. 3. to feel, to remain, to become, to sound, to taste, to stay, to seem, to grow, to smell, to appear, to look, to be (is, am, are, was, were, be, being, been) 4. It's = It is 5. AMV/RA: People were flying kites in the park by our school. In the park located near our school, people were flying kites.

DAY 52: 1. In, <u>America, Is, Great, Spirit, St., Louis</u> 2. Because the flour is self-rising, we'll use it. 3. A. pronoun B. adjective (Many tables) 4. A. clause (<u>we ate</u>) B. phrase (prepositional phrase) 5. AMV/RA: Used as a centerpiece, the daisies on the table are fresh. The fresh daisies on the table serve as a centerpiece.

DAY 53: 1. On, Chessa's, Choice, Eagle, Airlines 2. You're to leave at 6:00 A.M. for London, England. 3. driven; <u>must have driven</u> 4. Mr. Tomshack 5. AMV/RA: The blue shirt hanging on the hanger needs to be ironed. The blue shirt that needs to be ironed is hanging on a hanger.

DAY 54: 1. The, Protestant, Methodist, Sunday 2. Tony asked, "Mother, may I have some money?" 3. bursting 4. anything 5. AMV/RA: The painting of the artist's father won first place at the art fair. That painting, the one of the artist's father, won first place in the art fair.

DAY 55: 1. We, King's, World, Tapa, Rose, Gardens, Los, Angeles 2. Rule A: Enter quietly. / Rule B: Exit quietly. / Groceries: / -milk / -eggs / -bread 3. did 4. men's club 5. AMV/RA: When we used the tunnel through the mountain, we had to turn on our car's headlights. Entering the mountain tunnel, we turned on our headlights.

DAY 56: 1. My, Japanese 2. Did you read an article about the <u>Spruce Goose</u> in the newspaper, <u>Daily News</u>? 3. waitress's tip 4. A. heading B. inside address C. salutation or greeting D. body E. closing F. signature 5. AMV/RA: Her sister in Florida is a secretary who enjoys golf. Her sister, a Florida secretary, enjoys golf.

DAY 57: 1. Our, Roman 2. The children played; the parents watched television. 3. Your (Your bike) 4. not, so, quite, too, rather, very, somewhat 5. AMV/RA: Fallen snow has made the sidewalk wet and slippery. Because snow has fallen, the sidewalk is wet and slippery.

DAY 58: 1. The, Peoria, Columbus, Day, Parade 2. That patient has a heart problem; therefore, she walks daily. 3. phrase (A phrase doesn't contain both subject and verb.) 4. past, present 5. AMV/RA: The tall, curly-haired model works for Baron Modeling Agency. The model, tall and curly-haired, works for Baron Modeling Agency.

DAY 59: 1. The, Seminole, Indians, South 2. In today's newspaper, <u>City Chronicle,</u> Dad's picture is on p. 7. 3. she (subject) 4. Ms. Hart/Bob (The sentence can be inverted; **Ms. Hart and Bob were the winners of the race.**) 5. AMV/RA: For the bar graph assignment in math, a ruler was needed. A ruler was needed to draw a bar graph for the math assignment.

DAY 60: 1. I, Death, Hired, Man, Robert, Frost 2. Have you seen, Jack, any big blue balloons? 3. A. pronoun B. adjective (That blouse) 4. Grandma (One can mentally insert **to** before *Grandma.*) 5. AMV/RA: Although the tree that was planted last fall is thriving, it needs to be watered. The blossoming tree that was planted last fall needs to be watered.

DAY 61: 1. Have, Dr., Mrs., J., Jones, West, Ginger, Drive, El, Paso, Texas 2. Two-thirds of today's math class hasn't handed in homework. 3. brought; <u>must have brought</u> 4. toddler 5. AMV/RA: Mother was angry because a crayon melted in the heat on the car's back seat. Mother was angry; a crayon, left on the back seat, melted due to the heat.

DAY 62: 1. Some, African, Mexican 2. The poem entitled "If" was written by Rudyard Kipling, a great British author. 3. A. past B. present C. future 4. class's trophy 5. AMV/RA: Bill, a kindergartner, drew a picture of his dog. Bill, who is a kindergartner, drew a picture of his dog.

DAY 63: 1. Some, Native, Americans, Indian, <u>Bible</u> 2. Two-thirds of the math class hasn't turned in its assignment, Mary. 3. finishing 4. Tonight, there (You may wish, as a general review, to have students determine the verb phrase, **shall go**, and give its tense as future.) 5. AMV/RA: A lunch of pizza and milk will be served in our school cafeteria today. A lunch, pizza and milk, will be served in our school cafeteria today.

DAY 64: 1. In, June, Tompson, Tucson 2. My mild-mannered granny, the lady in the red dress, is not the culprit. 3. I (The sentence actually could read, "Bill is taller than I am.") 4. given; <u>had given</u> 5. AMV/RA: The boy , a blue-eyed blonde, was shivering from the cold. The blue-eyed, blonde-haired boy was shivering.

DAY 65: 1. For, Danish, Rainmist, Belgian 2. After Tate's last run, he struck out. (!) 3. its 4. A. declarative B. exclamatory C. interrogative D. imperative 5. AMV/RA: After the frog sat on the rock, he jumped swiftly into the water. Leaving the rock, the frog jumped swiftly into the water.

DAY 66: 1. Some, Oriental, Chang's, Chinese, Furniture 2. On Tues., Feb. 28, 1988, we celebrated Peter's birthday. 3. too, somewhat, rather, quite, very, not, so 4. chosen; <u>has been chosen</u> 5. AMV/RA: The hot, sunny day found us swimming in our pool and Mother baking in the kitchen. While we swam in our pool on the hot, sunny day, Mother baked in the kitchen.

DAY 67: 1. Has, Father, Y.M.C.A. 2. "What on earth," asked Kyle, "are you doing?" 3. <u>students</u> and <u>teacher</u> <u>May leave</u> 4. A. heading B. salutation or greeting C. body D. closing E. signature 5. AMV/RA: As the others watched, the monkey ate a banana while swinging limb to limb. The monkey, eating a banana, was swinging limb to limb; the others watched.

DAY 68: 1. Susan, Flair, Hair, Care, Wilson, Road 2. We need the following: lettuce, ice, syrup, and yogurt. 3. to look, to taste, to feel, to remain, to sound, to stay, to become, to seem, to grow, to appear, to smell, to be (is, am, are, was, were, be, being, been) 4. middle, assembly 5. AMV/RA: Jane loves pepperoni pizza; her brother hates all pizza. Although Jane loves all pizza, especially pepperoni, her brother hates all pizza.

DAY 69: 1. My, Grandmother, Billings, Yosemite, National, Park, California 2. My dad, the man in the red sweater, is also those boys' coach. 3. interjection 4. Those, red, the, planter 5. AMV/RA: The blue wool sweater was torn by Jill Fox. Jill Fox tore a blue wool sweater.

DAY 70: 1. Did, Buddhism, China, Far, East 2. Lila's report was entitled "Mars: A Great Planet." 3. A. Greek B. Dutch C. French D. Tonka 4. phrase 5. AMV/RA: The calendar hanging on the wall pictures George Washington. A picture of George Washington is on the calendar that is hanging on the wall.

DAY 71: 1. On, Monday, U., S., House, Representatives 2. The ex-teacher, in fact, retired to Duluth, Minn., last summer. 3. A. imperative B. declarative C. interrogative D. exclamatory E. declarative 4. Today (when), very (to what extent), cautiously (how), away (where) 5. AMV/RA: Both the fitness and stamp classes meet at four o'clock on Tuesdays; I have to make a choice. Because the fitness and stamp classes meet at four o'clock on Tuesdays, I have to decide which to attend.

DAY 72: 1. The, Regal, Motor, Company, Detroit 2. "Deka," exclaimed the teacher, "you scored 100%.(!)" 3. me (indirect object) 4. boys' golf clubs 5. AMV/RA: The cake, chocolate with peanut butter frosting, is for Laylah's tenth birthday. The chocolate cake with peanut butter frosting is for Laylah's tenth birthday.

DAY 73: 1. We, Charta, Ski, Resort, Fairfield, Pennsylvania 2. Because we are studying insects, we'll read the chapter entitled "Flying Insects."

3. A. Tomas (To prove it, turn the sentence around: **Tomas was the first person in line**.) 4. A. action B. linking (Milk **tastes** sour. Milk **was** sour.) 5. AMV/RA: While Dad is grocery shopping and Mom is at her office, I shall play tennis. Dad's grocery shopping, Mom's at her office, and I'm going to play tennis.

DAY 74: 1. An, Po, Queen, Chinese 2. Kaleena Drang, D. D. S., will speak about decay, plaque, and flossing. 3. hamsters 4. <u>s</u> (glasses), <u>x</u> (boxes), <u>z</u>(buzzes), <u>sh</u> (dishes), <u>ch</u> (churches) 5. AMV/RA: The students, enjoying an outside art class, sketched a landscape. In an outside art class, most students enjoyed sketching landscapes.

DAY 75: 1. The, Battle, Shiloh, Civil, War, American 2. Larry's sculpture is the tall, curved one. 3. A. calves B. mustards C. mice D. griefs (The word, *grieves*, serves as a verb, not a noun.) E. losses 4. and, but, or 5. AMV/RA: Mary's snowy-white lamb followed her everywhere she went. Mary's lamb, little and white-fleeced, followed her everywhere.

DAY 76: 1. During, Elizabethan, William, Shakespeare, A, Midsummer, Night's, Dream 2. Dear Jan, / I'll see you on Monday, Dec. 5th, 2005, at 2:00 P.M. / Your friend, / Sarah 3. A. adjective B. pronoun C. adjective D. pronoun 4. A. exclamatory B. imperative C. interrogative D. declarative 5. AMV/RA: The lovely bouquet of orchids was for the bride. The bridal bouquet of orchids was lovely.

DAY 77: 1. Ode, Grecian, Urn, John, Donne 2. The C. H. Jobe Co. moved to 24 Bilt St., Lincoln, Neb. 3. hoarse 4. dependent 5. AMV/RA: Because John was the outstanding salesperson in his company, he won a prize, a trip to Hawaii. John, an outstanding salesperson for his company, won a trip to Hawaii.

DAY 78: 1. The, Salk, Dr., Jonas, Salk, St., Jerome's, Hospital 2. The story, "All Summer in a Day," was read by Mrs. Lark's class. 3. their (The antecedent is *speakers*.) 4. majority, voters, recall, official 5. AMV/RA: The baby, given a pink stuffed bunny for Easter, laughed and chewed on its ear. The baby was given a pink stuffed bunny for Easter; she laughed and chewed on its ear.

DAY 79: 1. My, Anita, Arabic, Iranian 2. "This spot, quiet and secluded, is my favorite," said Jim. 3. babies' toy 4. come 5. AMV/RA: For a World War I study, some pupils are doing projects while others are writing research papers. Although some students are doing projects for a World War I unit, others are writing research papers.

DAY 80: 1. During, James, Monroe's, Era, Good, Feeling 2. Basketball isn't difficult, but I'd rather play tennis. 3. dependent 4. man sat 5. AMV/RA: As we sat throwing pebbles into the lake, a train sped by. Sitting on a rock, we threw pebbles into a lake as a train sped by.

DAY 81: The, German, Asian 2. If you're going, bring half of the food. 3. n't, no, He didn't have any money. **OR** He had no money. 4. Mom 5. AMV/RA: Because Tim has measles, a childhood disease, he will not be in school. The childhood disease of measles will keep Tim from attending school.

DAY 82: 1. While, San, Francisco, Golden, Gate, Bridge 2. The article entitled "Food Funds" appeared in the newspaper, The Star Republic. 3. you (Inverted sentence: **You will be the first choice.**) 4. A, soft, the, early (Note to students that **calmly** is an adverb. Although **early** can be an adverb, early is an adjective here.) 5. AMV/RA: When in San Diego, we went sailing, fishing, and surfing. Our San Diego jaunt included sailing, fishing, and surfing.

DAY 83: 1. The, Cape, Good, Hope, Africa 2. Deana remarked, "I like the mountains in Virginia." 3. Yesterday, n't, early 4. A. pronoun B. adjective (that briefcase) C. pronoun 5. AMV/RA: The abandoned car at the bottom of the hill had been stolen. The car that was stolen had been abandoned at the bottom of the hill.

DAY 84: 1. When, Captain, Hale, Grand, Canyon, Japanese 2. "Sally, I don't have any," replied the mother. 3. clause 4. have 5. AMV/RA: John enjoyed Peru, especially the Andes Mountains; in fact, John wants to return again next summer. Because John enjoyed the Andes Mountains of Peru, he wants to return to Peru next summer.

DAY 85: 1. The, Lady, Tramp, Fox, Theater 2. Ellen Smith, D.D.S., has her office in the Tracton Building. 3. clause (independent clause: <u>bread is</u>) 4. we (The word, **travel,** has been omitted after the pronoun. The sentence could read: **Those hikers travel faster than we travel.**) 5. AMV/RA: Miniature, porcelain, gold-edged music boxes are offered for sale.

DAY 86: 1. During, Labor, Day, Eastern 2. They're absolutely right; however, Prof. Lee may disagree. 3. vacationers, coast, San Diego 4. A. present B. past C. future 5. AMV/RA: Karen's parents who are vegetarians don't eat meat; however, Karen enjoys hot dogs. Although Karen's parents are vegetarians, Karen enjoys hot dogs.

DAY 87: 1. Is, Golton's, Colombian, Hungry-Boy, Restaurant 2. Jess, haven't you met Mr. Cline, the dance instructor? 3. two dogs' bowls 4. most gentle (superlative form) 5. AMV/RA: Not only were the blueberry pancakes and toast burned, but also the eggs were soggy. In addition to the soggy eggs, the blueberry pancakes and toast were burned.

DAY 88: 1. Chris, I, Flax, Taxi, Service, John, Wayne, International, Airport, Orange, County, Calif. 2. On June 7, 1995, my parents visited Idaho, Ohio, and Utah. 3. A. can't B. won't C. don't D. I'd E. she'll 4. My (pronoun used as an adjective), old, rusted, a, bright, green 5. AMV/RA: The pin-striped, English, woolen suit was purchased for her business conference. For a business conference, the woman purchased a woolen, pin-striped suit that had been made in England.

DAY 89: 1. Our, Mayflower, Compact, Pilgrims', America 2. "There's not a <u>t</u> in <u>pebble</u>," said the teacher. 3. most dangerously 4. flying 5. AMV/RA: After we ski and sled, we will ice skate. We will go skiing, sledding, and ice skating, respectively.

DAY 90: 1. Sugar, Castaway's, Kosey's, Cafe 2. When the car's red light came on, Jamilah stopped. 3. A. adverb B. preposition (out the door) C. adverb D. preposition (in the attic) 4. A. movies B. ladies C. monkeys D. proofs E. mothers-in-law 5. AMV/RA: Working long hours, the nurses administer medication and consult with doctors. During the long, arduous hours of employment, nurses not only administer medication but also consult with doctors.

DAY 91: 1. I. Great Battles / A. American victories / 1. Naval battles / 2. Skirmishes on land / B. Triumphs of the British / 2. I won't go; Tammy, please stay with me. 3. already, nearly, together 4. A. heading B. salutation (greeting) C. body D. closing E. signature 5. AMV/RA: For my birthday next week, Grandpa, as usual, will send money, and Mom will prepare my favorite meal.

DAY 92: 1. The, Days, Our, Serenity, English 2. Mrs. Hester L. Strong / 222 E. Irvine Blvd. / Tustin, CA 3. myself, herself, himself, yourself, itself, ourselves, themselves 4. more adorable (comparative form) 5. AMV/RA: The toy truck's dead batteries need to be replaced by ones in the drawer. The toy truck won't operate due to dead batteries; fortunately, new batteries are in the drawer.

DAY 93: 1. My dear friend, / See me at tomorrow's Hispanic fair. / Yours truly, / Sean 2. Who's the author of the poem, "The Raven"? 3. auxiliary 4. <u>robins</u> <u>perched</u> and <u>flew</u> 5. AMV/RA: When Mia uses her four baby teeth to bite her brother, he just laughs. Mia's brother only laughs when she uses her four baby teeth to bite him.

DAY 94: 1. The, <u>U.S.S.</u>, <u>Constitution</u>, Boston, Harbor, War 2. Running down the street, the dog knocked over Mark's bike. 3. she (Predicate nominative: The inverted sentence will read, **She will be the speaker.**) 4. is, am, are, was, were, be, being, been, has, have, had, do, does, did, may, must, might, will, shall, would, should, could, can 5. AMV/RA: The cracked Italian floor tile with geometric designs needs to be replaced. The cracked floor tile, the Italian one with geometric designs, needs to be replaced.

DAY 95: 1. The, Thanksgiving, <u>Of</u>, <u>Pilgrims</u>, <u>We</u>, <u>Are</u>, <u>Proud</u> 2. Armistice Day, also known as Veteran's* Day, is Nov. 11.
   *One will see this also written **Veterans'**.
3. <u>balloon</u> <u>had drifted</u> and <u>was soaring</u> 4. A. direct object B. adverb C. predicate nominative D. direct object 5. AMV/RA: The shrill sound of the ambulance's siren awakened us as it sped by. We were awakened by the shrill siren of an ambulance speeding by.

DAY 96: 1. We, Holuba, Hall, Penn, State, University 2. "The low, rolling hills were a photographer's dream," remarked Marion. 3. appositive 4. best 5. AMV/RA: The golfers, meeting at 6 A.M., found the course already filled and decided to try another one. The golfers, finding the course filled at 6 A.M., decided to try another course.

DAY 97: 1. <u>The</u>, Great, <u>Gatsby</u>, American, Fitzgerald 2. Susan, take this for me; I need to leave now.(!) 3. <u>Many</u> <u>had been eaten</u> (*Apples* is the object of the preposition.) 4. more slowly 5. AMV/RA: The blooming red and white petunias were planted two months ago. Although the red and white petunias were only planted two months ago, they are blooming.

DAY 98: 1. The, McLean, Lutheran, Albany, New, York 2. We will meet, without a doubt, to discuss Mrs. Smith's account. 3. <u>ducks</u> and <u>birds</u> <u>are enjoying</u> 4. ladies 5. AMV/RA: My aunt, a dental hygienist who cleans my teeth, recommends that I brush more often. My aunt, a dental hygienist, not only cleans my teeth, but also recommends that I brush them more often.

DAY 99: 1. During, University, Florida, Jacksonville, Naval, Air, Station 2. At 9:15 A.M. on Sept.. 7, I'll see the movie, <u>Tiger Eyes</u>. 3. A. future B. present C. past 4. A. abstract B. abstract C. concrete 5. AMV/RA: When our class went to the zoo last week, we enjoyed the giraffes the most. Visiting the zoo last week, our class enjoyed the giraffes the most.

DAY 100: 1. A, St., Paul, Police, Dept. 2. His brother-in-law works in Topeka, Kansas, twice a year. 3. ridden; <u>has ridden</u> 4. storm, side, road 5. AMV/RA: Our scout leaders, Mr. and Mrs. Burns, have invited Deputy Jones to speak on desert survival at Wednesday's meeting. Our scout troop, under the leadership of Mr. and Mrs. Burns, will meet Wednesday; at that time, Deputy Jones will speak to us about desert survival.

DAY 101: 1. Is, <u>Queen</u>, <u>Anne</u>, British, American 2. The child's shoe broke; her mother repaired it. 3. direct object = talk; indirect object = them 4. AMV/RA: A. Charles B. Redmont Elementary School C. Fabulous Food Restaurant 5. AMV/RA: During the cold, windy storm, rain fell heavily and filled the road with puddles. As rain fell heavily, filling the road with puddles, a cold wind blew.

DAY 102: 1. The, Strait, Gibraltar, Suez, Canal, Mediterranean, Sea 2. Didn't her name appear on the list as Markle, Susan? 3. sneaked; <u>might have sneaked</u> (**To sneak** is a regular verb.) 4. I (subject = <u>others</u> and <u>I</u>) 5. AMV/RA: Pine trees were covered with snow that had fallen throughout the night. The snow, having fallen throughout the night, covered the pines.

DAY 103: 1. At, Gore, Meadow, School, Ms., Jones, The, Midnight, Ride, Paul, Revere 2. Your decision, I'm afraid, will create lasting problems. 3. A. direct object B. indirect object C. object of the preposition 4. Some, loaded, fishing, the, luminous, deep 5. AMV/RA: Scampering in the forest, squirrels gathered and stored nuts in a tree, but voices suddenly frightened them. Before voices in the forest startled them, the squirrels had been scampering about gathering and storing nuts.

DAY 104: 1. The, French, Bavarian, Duck, Delight, Diner 2. When the children's playground is finished, let's go there. 3. Sue and Tom's pet 4. The, fallen, brown, crisp, fragrant 5. AMV/RA: An alligator living in the Okefenokee Swamp displayed his teeth as a warning to an intruder. Warning an intruder, an alligator in the Okefenokee Swamp showed his teeth.

DAY 105: 1. One, French, Manet, Brioche, Pears 2. Susan Lang, a German-born citizen, spoke at our riders' club meeting. 3. A. present B. future C. past 4. A. heading B. salutation (greeting) C. body D. closing E. signature 5. AMV/RA: During her European vacation, Cousin Gwen bought me a feather bed, which is like a huge pillow that conforms to your body.

DAY 106: 1. Were, Comanche, Indians, Chief, Parker, Oklahoma 2. In the book, <u>Silas Marner</u>, was the miser's life self-indulgent? 3. A. adverb (**Slowly** tells how Jane walks.) B. adjective (slow walker) C. adverb (**Better** tells how Bob drew it.) D. adjective (better swimmer) 4. A. DC B. IC C. DC D. IC 5. AMV/RA: Marv's eye is swollen and bloodshot from an eye infection. An eye infection has caused Marv's eye to swell and become bloodshot.

DAY 107: 1. Is, Park, Presbyterian, Church, Blake, Street, Pastor, Smith 2. Millie said, "Jane's brother-in-law wasn't re-elected as governor." 3. me (object of the preposition = to my brother and me) 4. <u>One; had planted</u> and <u>is hoping</u> 5. AMV/RA: Although Sue was elected class president today, I voted for Ted. Sue was elected class president today; however, I voted for Ted.

DAY 108: 1. In, Religions, World, Israelite, Hindu 2. On Fri., Sept. 8, Tom and Alice's stories will be read on television at 8 A.M. 3. A. adjective (several pants) B. pronoun C. adjective (several crews) 4. The child never wants any. **OR** The child wants none. 5. AMV/RA: The blue kitchen telephone was off the hook, and a beeping sound was coming from it. Because the blue kitchen telephone was off the hook, a beeping sound was being emitted.

DAY 109: 1. I, St., Valentine's, Day, February 2. Marie said, "Mother, may I go to the dance?" 3. loudly (adverb telling **how**) 4. is, am, are, was, were, be, being, been, has, have, had, do, does, did, may, must, might, shall, will, can, should, could, would 5. AMV/RA: Mrs. Kerr, the president of the P.T.A. who was elected outstanding leader, has a fourth-grade daughter. Mrs. Kerr, named outstanding leader as president of our school's P.T.A., has a daughter who is in fourth grade.

DAY 110: 1. At, St., Paul's, Winter, Carnival 2. A spacious, elegant lobby opened onto a well-lighted veranda. 3/4.

STREET ADDRESS
CITY, STATE ZIP
TODAY'S DATE

DEAR

_____
_____
_____

CLOSING, (lined up with heading)
SIGNATURE

5. AMV/RA: Take the stamps and envelopes from the desk, place the stamps on the envelopes, and mail them. The stamps and envelopes are in the desk drawer; mail the envelopes after placing stamps on them.

DAY 111: 1. The, James, Mary, British, Royal, Dockyard 2. "You're, without a doubt, the team's best player!" exclaimed Ned. 3. A. fell B. do, does C. chose D. will run 4. floor, sofa, trash 5. AMV/RA: The large black and white sign announcing "Sal's Pizzeria" is lighted after dark. The "Sal's Pizzeria" sign, the large black and white one, is lighted after dark.

DAY 112: 1. Our, Independence, Day, Lake, Powell 2. If you cross your t's in the word, letter, you'll have a perfect paper, Paul. 3. A. common B. common C. proper D. common E. proper 4. interjection 5. AMV/RA: Breaking a fingernail while removing a staple from her paper, Sharon cried out in disgust. Because Sharon broke a fingernail while removing a staple from a paper, she cried out in disgust.

DAY 113: 1. The, Tory, Party, American, Revolution 2. We're going into the teachers' lounge for a workbook. 3. their; antecedent = trees 4. A. adverb B. preposition (**down** the street) C. adverb (**down** ~~into the hole~~) 5. AMV/RA: Pliers on the workbench and various tools lying on the floor were indications that Karen is in the midst of making furniture again. Karen is in the midst of making furniture again; pliers and other tools are lying around.

DAY 114: 1. Have, Tropical, Garden, Zoo, Seventh, Street 2. 27 Poe Rd. / Columbus, Ohio / May 7, 2009 / Dear Bob, / I'll send you the book, Tex, soon.* / Your friend, / Janet 3. luckier 4. Either/or 5. AMV/RA: As the team, hopeful of victory, ran onto the field, the crowd stood and cheered.
   *Some teach that a one-word appositive does not require commas.

DAY 115: 1. 77 Dree St. / San Diego, CA / June 2, 2009 / To my best friend, / I will meet you at Kennedy International Airport. / Love always, / Mickey 2. Is Capt. Kirk aboard the Enterprise on the television show, Star Trek? 3. come; has come 4. I (predicate nominative: **Mrs. Tils and I are the next speakers.**) 5. AMV/RA: Uncle Ted enjoys driving both the tractor and the red sports car that are housed in the garage.

DAY 116: 1. I. Furniture / A. Beds / 1. Types of beds / 2. Care of beds / B. Chairs / II. Belongings /   2. The M. C. Kraft Co. has moved to 33 Trellis Dr., St. Louis, Missouri. 3. Our, favorite, a, creative 4. Bill or family Should have gone 5. AMV/RA: The gift, wrapped in shiny red foil, had a pink taffeta bow with red lollipops entwined.

DAY 117: 1. Jo, Ellen, Southwest, Indian, Latin, America 2. At 2:00 P.M.,* I need the following: paint, three brushes, and two rollers.
*The comma is optional.
3. I, he, she, we, they, you, it, who 4. Yesterday, quite, late 5. AMV/RA: The small wicker basket was filled with pine cones and dried flowers. Pine cones lined the bottom of the small, wicker basket filled with dried flowers.

DAY 118: 1. After, Nagasaki, Shinto, Japan 2. A. <u>Hamlet</u> B. "If" C. <u>Marie</u> D. "Westward Ho" 3. <u>play</u> and <u>story</u> <u>were</u> 4. phrase (There is neither subject nor verb.) 5. AMV/RA: Enjoying the soft, mushy mud, the toddlers played by making mud pies and smearing them on the wall. The toddlers, playing in the soft, mushy mud, made mud pies and smeared them on the wall.

DAY 119: 1. In, Greek, Ares, Athena 2. "This idea, in fact," said Bob, "wasn't suggested." 3. <u>cook</u>, <u>waiter</u>, or <u>hostess</u> <u>lose</u> 4. A. interrogative B. imperative C. declarative D. exclamatory 5. AMV/RA: Because rain had fallen, the streets were flooded, and the river was overflowing. Two days of continuous rain produced flooded streets and an overflowing river.

DAY 120: 1. The, China, Hsia, Dynasty 2. Her mother-in-law, the lady in the pink blouse, is Joan Davis, R.N. 3. I (than I **sing**) 4. fragment (**Subject** is missing.) 5. AMV/RA: While Jill watched television, her sister read a book and her mother spoke on the telephone. Jill watched television, her sister read a book, and her mother talked on the telephone.

DAY 121: 1. In, English, Gift, Magi, O., Henry 2. A. <u>Spruce Goose</u> B. "Jack and Jill" C. <u>Health and Wealth</u> D. "Food to You" 3. slowly 4. is, am, are, was, were, be, being, been, do, does, did, has, have, had, may, must, might, can, could, will, would, shall, should 5. AMV/RA: At the annual carnival, we saw a clown making funny animals from balloons. A clown who makes funny animals from balloons performed at the annual carnival.

DAY 122: 1. A. "A Walk in the Park" B. "The Yellow Rose of Texas" C. <u>I Know What You Did Last Summer</u> D. <u>One Flew over the Cuckoo's Nest</u> 2. "Life's pleasures are exciting at age forty-two," said Lieut. Hine. 3. puppies, backs, rug 4. me (object of the preposition: to Ms. Sims and **to** me) 5. AMV/RA: Because the father had promised to take the children for ice cream, they waited patiently while he dressed. Having been promised to be taken for ice cream by their father, the children waited patiently for him to dress.

DAY 123: 1. Will, Mother, Senator, Jobe, U., S., Senate, Washington, D., C. 2. The book, <u>Designed by God</u>, discusses a woman's life. 3. his (***Everyone*** is singular.) 4. ridden; <u>has</u> <u>ridden</u> 5. AMV/RA: During the race, the girl sprained her ankle and couldn't finish. During the race, the girl fell and sprained her ankle; therefore, she didn't finish the race.

DAY 124: 1. The, Organization, American, States, Central, American 2. The boss, the coworker, and Joan's father attended the meeting. 3. A. adverb B. preposition (near Omaha) C. adverb (near **to me** = prepositional phrase) 4. A, serious, archaeological 5. AMV/RA: On the patio, a bee buzzed while a black and yellow butterfly fluttered. As the bee buzzed, a black and yellow butterfly fluttered on the patio.

DAY 125: 1. During, Renaissance, Johann, Gutenberg 2. Sen. Barkin's address is 21 Dale Ln., Houston, Texas, in the summer. 3. Sue's, school's 4. A. phrase (prepositional phrase) B. clause (independent clause) C. clause (dependent clause) 5. AMV/RA: John's mustard-stained vest was the result of his dripping mustard from a hot dog. John spilled mustard from a hot dog onto his vest; the vest, therefore, had become stained.

DAY 126: 1. The, French, Protestants, Huguenots 2. I haven't any time now, but let's meet at Tom's house later. 3. A. moose B. supplies C. commanders in chief D. geese E. flashes 4. climb 5. AMV/RA: The red juicy apples hanging in the tree are in danger of rotting and need to be picked. Because the red juicy apples are in danger of rotting, they need to be picked.

DAY 127: 1. The, Blake, Junior, High, School, Harman, Hall 2. A. <u>Wheel of Fortune</u> B. "Millie" C. "Hair Care" 3. AMV/RA: abstract - love, beauty, peace, patience; concrete - pen, wall, windshield, person 4. driven; <u>was driven</u> 5. AMV/RA: Marlo had used the broken yellow pen to write a report. The pen, broken and yellow, had been used by Marlo to write a report.

DAY 128: 1. The, Girl, Scout, Troop, Garden, Grove, Freeway 2. A news update revealed that Gov. Doe had a two-third's majority. 3. too, quite, very, so, rather, somewhat, not 4. <u>Both</u> (**Of the skaters** is a prepositional phrase and should be crossed out.) <u>fell</u>, <u>arose</u> 5. AMV/RA: The mountains, tall and majestic, their peaks covered with snow, were a beautiful sight with the sun glistening on them. The tall, majestic, snow-covered mountains glistened in the sunshine.

DAY 129: 1. Does, Skyline, Drive, Appalachian, Mountains 2. This isn't the recipe's amount; you need one-third cup of butter. 3. direct object = puppy; indirect object = sister 4. beauty, serenity, place, wonder 5. AMV/RA: Last week's rain and the favorable spring weather have caused our daisies to bloom. Our blooming daisies have resulted from favorable spring weather and recent rain.

DAY 130: 1. The, Hopi, Indian, Southwest 2. An article, Braille on the Trail," appeared in the magazine, <u>Hiking Adventures.</u> 3. to taste, to smell, to feel, to look, to appear, to stay, to remain, to become, to seem, to sound, to grow, to be (is, am, are, was, were, be, being, been) 4. A, gracious, restaurant, a, secluded 5. AMV/RA: I will change the hallway light that has been burned out for two weeks. Because the hallway light has been burned out for two weeks, I will change the bulb.

DAY 131: 1. Has, Rhyme, Ancient, Mariner 2. After we've been to the store, we'll eat lunch, rest, and golf. 3. is, am, are, was, were, be, being, been, do, does, did, has, have, had, may, might, must, will, would, shall, should, can, could 4. ponies |galloped

across |field the

5. AMV/RA: New construction of the home began with the pouring of the cement; the carpenters will start tomorrow. Because the cement was poured for the new home under construction, the carpenters will start tomorrow.

DAY 132: 1. Dawn's, Siamese, Officer, Dobb, Monday 2. Miss James asked, "Why aren't we finished, class?" 3. Suddenly (when), rather (to what extent), out (where), away (where) 4. A. drink(s), drank, (had) drunk B. freeze(s), froze, (had) frozen C. know(s), knew, (had) known 5. AMV/RA: The mother, walking into the living room, stumbled over the toy that the toddler had abandoned in favor of a puzzle. The toddler, fascinated by a puzzle, abandoned the toy in the middle of the living room; his mother promptly stumbled over it.

DAY 133: 1. The, Dree, Middle, School, Presidents', Day, Memorial, Day 2. In March, 1990, we moved to Dad's hometown, Nashville, Tenn. 3. him (direct object) 4. walking 5. AMV/RA: Because the child broke his arm in a fall from a tree, a doctor at the hospital put a cast on it. Having fallen from a tree and broken his arm, the child was taken to a hospital where a doctor placed the arm in a cast.

DAY 134: 1. Is, Congressman, Pedd, Arbor, Day 2. No, we won't stay, and I'm, without a doubt, relieved. 3. possessive = her , antecedent = diver 4. The, angry, trembling, that 5. AMV/RA: The runners, excited about the relay race, were competing for a class trophy. Competing for a class trophy, the runners were excited about the relay race.

DAY 135: 1. The, Jewish, Community, Center, Dallas 2. Rule A: NO HITTING / Rule B: NO SHOVING 3. A. go(es), went, (had) gone B. lie(s), lay, (had) lain C. burst(s), burst, (had) burst 4. AMV/RA: Take this. Please remind me. 5. AMV/RA: The sea gull glided over the ocean, swooped low over the beach, and landed on a jagged rock. Gliding over the ocean, the sea gull swooped low over the beach and landed on a jagged rock.

DAY 136: 1. A. Raindrops, Keep, Falling, Head B. Everything, Is, Negotiable C. Don't, Sit, Under, Apple, Tree, Anyone, Else, Me 2. Our principal, Tom Nast, makes short, snappy speeches. 3. twins' book 4. A. past B. none C. future D. present 5. AMV/RA: Mrs. Lart, an employee of an electronics company, was transferred with her family from Ohio to Texas. Working for an electronics company, Mrs. Lart and her family were transferred from Ohio to Texas.

DAY 137: 1. A, Polynesian, Yang 2. Chanda said, "Maria and Kesi, my cousins, can't visit on Friday, June 12." or
  Chanda said, "Maria and Kesi, my cousins can't visit on Friday, June 12."
3. present and past 4. direct object = tools; indirect objects = Dad, me 5. AMV/RA: A new, self-correcting typewriter was purchased and placed in our classroom. When the new, self-correcting typewriter was purchased, it was placed in our classroom.

DAY 138: 1. At, Daisy, Food, Company, Polish, Lasco 2. Ms. Jones, our ex-teacher, now works for Gat Co., 52 Elm St. 3. Our*, older, those, large, outstanding
        *pronoun used as an adjective
4. A. preposition (up the stairs) B. adverb 5. AMV/RA: A slowworm, a European lizard, has a smooth, snakelike body that is two to three feet long. Although a slowworm is a European lizard, it has a two to three feet long smooth, snakelike body.

DAY 139: 1.   45 Trow Street
                                            Salem, Oregon
                                            July 9

        Dear little Ann,

2. Mrs. Dil, may I have the following: a comb, a scarf, and a pin? 3. better 4. I (subject) 5. AMV/RA: The soft, chewy rolls had just been taken from the oven and brushed with melted butter. After the soft, chewy rolls were taken from the oven, they were brushed with melted butter.

DAY 140: 1. The, Autobiography, Mother, Glone, Enterprises 2. "The fort's gate is closed but will open at 8:30 A.M.," said the guard. 3. <u>father</u> <u>will be</u> 4. most calmly 5. AMV/RA: Having dropped hair dye on the new tile and creating a permanent stain, the lady shrieked in frustration. The lady dropped hair dye on the new tile which created a permanent stain; therefore, she shrieked in frustration.

DAY 141: 1. The, J., O., Cone, Co., St., Patrick's, Day, Irish 2. Although the club's name was changed, it meets regularly. 3. A. adverb B. preposition (around the room) C. adverb 4. A. clause B. phrase C. clause D. phrase 5. AMV/RA: The wide, rocky stream spilled water over a shallow waterfall. At the end of the wide, rocky stream was a waterfall.

DAY 142: 1. During, Labor, Day, European 2. Our team, Joe, has won the tournament, and we are now champions.(!) 3. A. American B. German C. Indonesian 4. Where, by 5. AMV/RA: The small plates that Dad needs for dinner are dirty; someone needs to wash them. The small, dirty plates are needed for Dad's dinner; someone needs to wash them.

DAY 143: 1. A. Cat, Hot, Tin, Roof B. I, Never, Promised, You, Rose, Garden C. Rudolph, Red-Nosed, Reindeer 2. Wow! I've been elected vice-president of our school's council! 3. is, am, are, was, were, be, being, been, do, does, did, have, has, had, may, must, might, will, would, shall, should, can, could 4. A. direct object B. predicate nominative 5. AMV/RA: When the teller lost a quarter which rolled behind a chair, a customer retrieved it. The teller, having lost a quarter behind a chair, was grateful that a customer retrieved it.

DAY 144: 1. The, Republican, Party, Dupre, Hotel, Paris 2. Casper asked, "Are you going to Yuma, Arizona, next week?" 3. A. object of the preposition (near **them**) B. predicate nominative (Chan and **he** are my favorites.) C. subject (Laylah and **I**) D. indirect object (mentally **"to" me**) E. direct object (**Us** is the object the dog licked.) 4. loudly (tells **how**) 5. AMV/RA: The daffodils, brilliant yellow flowers in red clay pots, were on sale for Mother's Day. On sale for Mother's Day in red clay pots were brilliant yellow daffodils.

Day 145: 1. The, Chicago, Museum, Art, Picasso
2/3.
         21 Roe Blvd.
         Boise, Idaho   **A. heading**
         Sept. 21, 2006

Dear Sue,   **B. salutation (greeting)**
     We've so much to discuss. When you're here, we'll talk about our plans.   **C. body**
           Love,   **D. closing**
           Kathy   **E. signature**
4. gone; <u>must have gone</u> 5. AMV/RA: The smooth, chocolate-colored tile was laid on the floor by two experts.

DAY 146: 1. Is, Pastor, Lave, Lutheran, Rye, Road 2. Mr. Crem frantically took an exam; however, he passed it. (!) 3. honesty, calmness, pressure, approval. 4. known; <u>might have known</u> 5. AMV/RA: As the child darted into the street after the tennis ball, the father yelled for the child to stop. The father, seeing his child dart into the street after a tennis ball, yelled for him(her) to stop.

DAY 147: 1. During, Hurricane, Anne, Gulf, Mexico 2. Her dad, the man in the gray pin-striped suit, is Prof. Hobb. 3. A. preposition (over the fence) B. adverb (**where**) C. adverb (*in the morning* = a prepositional phrase) 4. A. linking (predicate adjective = tired) B. action C. linking (predicate nominative = car) 5. AMV/RA: Both the groups of boys and girls went to the mall; however, the girls went to the theater there. Although both groups, the boys and the girls, went to the mall, the girls elected to go to the movie theater.

DAY 148: 1. I, Bev, Lincoln, Memorial, Alamo 2. The class of '99 held its reunion; many attended. 3. A. well B. good C. well 4. swimming 5. AMV/RA: The old, corroded diamond ring, found in a gutter, was taken to a jeweler for repair. Although the old, diamond ring found in a gutter was corroded, it was taken to a jeweler for repair.

DAY 149: 1. The, Iberian, Peninsula, Portugal, Spain 2. Your suggestion, as a matter of fact, Shawn, was an innovative, acceptable one. 3. friend, Bill Cole, mechanic, city, Charleston 4. A. clause (<u>I were</u>) B. phrase C. phrase 5. AMV/RA: Because March was cold, rainy, and windy, it was our least favorite month. The cold, rainy, windy month of March was our least favorite.

DAY 150: 1. During, Battle, San, Jacinto, Texas 2. A. "Fossils" B. <u>How Great Thou Art</u> C. "We Are Family" 3. waitress's tips 4. A. bring(s), brought, brought B. love(s), loved, loved C. run(s), ran, run 5. AMV/RA: Because a pizza party was being planned for Paula's birthday, invitations were sent to her friends. The invitations that were purchased and sent to Paula's friends are for a pizza party in honor of her birthday.

DAY 151: 1. Does, Darn, Paint, Co., Peppy, Girl 2. His uptight (or up tight) attitude isn't usual, and he's usually calm and relaxed. 3. A. direct object B. subject C. predicate nominative 4. AMV/RA: to bring, to seem, to jump, to deliver 5. AMV/RA: Although Dr. Vargas is my podiatrist, a foot doctor, he shares a building with my aunt, Dr. Morgan. Dr. Morgan, my aunt, shares a building with Dr. Vargas, a podiatrist who serves as my foot doctor.

DAY 152: 1. A. "Death of a Hired Man" B. <u>The Tale of Two Cities</u> C. "The Wisdom of Life" D. "The Secret Life of Walter Mitty" 2. It's a full-page picture of Lassie; I'd like one. 3. A. present = eat(s), past = ate, future = shall or will eat B. present = freeze(s), past = froze, future = shall or will freeze C. present = play(s), past = played, future = shall or will play 4. <u>many; wandered, devoured</u> 5. AMV/RA: Walking through forest, the deer stepped to the edge of the meadow, sniffed the air, and then ambled into the meadow.

DAY 153: 1. The, Andes, Mountains, Chile, Pacific 2. A. <u>U.S.S. Arizona</u> B. "The Fox and the Grapes" C. <u>Toys and Tots</u> 3. A. child's penny B. children's horse C. ladies' meeting 4. me (indirect object) 5. AMV/RA: The student, laughing at her silly answer, was reprimanded by a frowning teacher. The student laughed as she gave a silly answer; therefore, the teacher frowned and reprimanded her.

DAY 154: 1. A, Darway, Village, Keen, Drive 2. The boys, tired and disgruntled, counted only three-fourths of the coupons. 3. A. declarative B. exclamatory C. interrogative D. imperative 4. anything 5. AMV/RA: The chocolate ice cream bar that was purchased from the street vendor melted quickly in the hot sun. Due to the hot sun, the chocolate ice cream bar that was purchased from the street vendor melted quickly.

DAY 155: 1. In, Greek, Venus 2. Remove the extra <u>p</u> in <u>papper</u>, and it's correct, Fred. 3. anything 4. A. sentence B. run-on C. fragment 5. AMV/RA: Grandpa and Dad dug the trench for our yard's sprinkling system while Grandma and Mom laid the pipe. After Dad and Grandpa dug the trench for our yard's sprinkling system, Mom and Grandma laid the pipe.

DAY 156: 1. The, New, York, Philharmonic, Orchestra, Carnegie, Hall 2. "Tom, we need hay, horses, and a wagon for the hayride," said Cass. 3. her (antecedent = each) 4. An, oak, the, empty, twenty 5. AMV/RA: The cow, chewing its cud, meandered across the field as flies swarmed around her. With flies swarming around it, the cow chewed its cud and meandered across the field.

DAY 157: 1. The, Roman, Catholic, Christmas 2. The Poe Co. gave its honored, retiring employee a round-trip ticket to China. 3. A. octopi (or octopuses) B. crashes C. payments D. cries E. birthdays 4.

YOUR STREET ADDRESS
CITY, SATE ZIP
TODAY'S DATE

MAR COMPANY*
4 WEST ORG STREET
DETROIT, MICHIGAN ZIP

DEAR SIR: (or other acceptable answers)

*Accept other abbreviations if desired.

5. AMV/RA: Although Jan's younger brother invested in the stock market and made money, her other brother lost money doing so.

DAY 158: 1. Are, Villa, Nova, Apartments, Carp, Mountain 2. "Your bank, by the way, was closed for Washington's Birthday," remarked Jay. 3. plane, mountain, avalanche 4. A. independent clause B. dependent clause C. dependent clause 5. AMV/RA: Harry Tye's twenty dollar check for a book was sent through the mail. Harry Tye's twenty dollar check, payment for a book, was sent through the mail.

DAY 159: 1. The, Brim, Dog, Company, French, Brittany 2. Yipee! We girls scored twenty-two points at last night's game! 3. I (predicate nominative: **I was the first one to leave.**) 4. together, not, so, hard 5. AMV/RA: Sally, a student who worked her way through college as a waitress, graduated from college last May. Having worked her way through college as a waitress, Sally graduated last May.

DAY 160: 1. A, New, Mexico, Old, Glory, Veteran's, Day 2. His down-trodden view can't help Steve's problem. 3. A. fragment B. fragment C. not a fragment (sentence) 4. A. adverb B. adverb C. preposition 5. AMV/RA: The spacious townhouse that had two fireplaces and a skylight was purchased by the couple.

DAY 161: 1. The, Louisiana, Territory, Lewis, Clark, Shoshone, Indian, Sacajawea 2. Your well-written paper, however, has too many the's. 3. A. phrase (prepositional phrase) B. clause (dependent clause: they left) 4. n't, further, now 5. AMV/RA: We went to a movie, played cards, and then read. After the movie, we played cards and then read.

DAY 162: 1. In, Cape, Cod, New, England 2. Beth's article, "Life's Benefits," appeared on the thirty-second page of the magazine, Bronze. 3. some were praying 4. An, American, rose, a, shaded 5. AMV/RA: After the artist set up his easel and assembled his paints, he accidentally knocked them over. Having set up the easel and paints, the artist accidentally knocked them over.

DAY 163: 1. In, Biology I, Ms., Gore, Mendell's 2. Susan's father, I'm told, is an author, a professor, and a director. 3. raised; should have raised 4. he (The winner is **he.** PREDICATE NOMINATIVE: **He** is the winner.) 5. AMV/RA: In writing a prescription for penicillin, Dr. Hill asked the patient if she were allergic to the drug. Dr. Hill, writing a penicillin prescription, asked the patient if she were allergic to the drug.

DAY 164: 1. The, Gulf, Taranto, Mediterranean, Sea, Greeks (Some teach that *eighth century* should be capitalized.) 2. "Ken's family will arrive at 8 A.M. for the St. Jerome wedding," said the writer. 3. softer 4. lain 5. AMV/RA: The birthday card that had roses on the front and a poem inside was sent by Cal to his mom. Cal sent his mom a birthday card with roses on the front and a poem inside.

DAY 165: 1. The, English, Longson, Park, Piccadilly, Square 2. Joe's essay has too many and's; therefore, it scored a 3. 3. and, but, or 4. ball, donation, generosity 5. AMV/RA: The robin drank from a bird bath and flew to a nearby branch. Having drunk from a bird bath, the robin flew to a nearby branch.

DAY 166: 1. This, Nan, Mardi, Gras 2. On Oct. 23, 1991, her daughter was born in Baltimore, Md. 3. A. break(s), broke, broken B. show(s), showed, shown C. lie(s), lay, lain D. yell(s), yelled, yelled 4. A. sentence B. run-on C. fragment 5. AMV/RA: Although Ron received a large red wagon as a gift from his uncle, Ron doesn't play with it.

DAY 167: 1. When, Tracey, Chinese, The, Diary, Anne, Frank 2. Yes, we'll go to Montezuma's Castle, my friend. 3. Mr. Dobbs 4. A. phrase (prepositional phrase) B. phrase (participial phrase) C. clause (dependent clause) D. clause (independent clause) 5. AMV/RA: When Christy refused to do her stack of dirty laundry, her mom also refused to do it.

DAY 168: 1. Our, Lisa, Fob, Lane, St., Louis, Missouri 2. Carl is going to the state's boundary, but I'm going to Hartford, Conn. 3. wolf 4. AMV/RA: either/or, neither/nor, both/and 5. AMV/RA: A cricket in the family's new home was a sign of the probability of more crickets infiltrating the premises. When the members of the family saw a cricket in the kitchen, they knew that this was a sign of more to come.

DAY 169: 1. Did, Gov., Litton, Kiwanis, Club, American, Cuban 2. The U.S.S. Arizona, a ship at Pearl Harbor, Hawaii, was a victim of Japan's attack. 3. Afterward, n't, anywhere 4. me, him, her, us, them, you, it, whom 5. AMV/RA: Has anyone seen Mike's blue leather Banter Bank checkbook for which he is desperately searching?

DAY 170: 1. The, To, My, Wife, I, American 2. "His father-in-law, James Brooks, is Sen. J.J. Brooks," said Faye. 3. whom (object of the preposition) 4. A. preposition (object of preposition B. adverb (where) 5. AMV/RA: Although the librarian was upset by the lost book, she was pleased with its return. The librarian was upset that the book was lost; however, she was pleased when a student returned it.

DAY 171: 1. The, Royal, Dance, Academy, Singe, Nursing, Home, Cheyenne 2. "We'll give you," said Edna, "the up-to-date records of that camp." 3. Fresh, hot, onion, several, small, wicker 4. myself, himself, herself, yourself, ourselves, themselves 5. AMV/RA: Walking down a mile-long deserted lane, the children were picked up by a school bus. After the children walked a mile-long deserted lane, a school bus picked them up.

DAY 172: 1. The, New, Testament's, Matthew, Christian 2. This month's Bread and Bran magazine contains these recipes: muffins, raisin breads, and pancakes. 3. live (boys live), lives (Mary lives) 4. A. fragment B. sentence C. run-on 5. AMV/RA: Because the couple was celebrating their anniversary on a starry night, they ate a late dinner at an outdoor cafe and then browsed in several art galleries.

DAY 173: 1. The, Hellenistic, Age, Rome, Mediterranean, Sea 2. If you're going to the Lakers'* game, don't wear your two-tone jeans.
*also Laker's
3. AMV/RA: The boy, <u>your cousin,</u> is here. Have you seen Paul, <u>the new boy</u>? 4. softer 5. AMV/RA: On their European jaunt, her parents landed in London, ferried across the English Channel, and then traveled by train through France, Spain, and Portugal. Landing in London for their European vacation, the couple ferried across the English Channel and proceeded by train through France, Spain, and Portugal.

DAY 174: 1. The, Crusades, Muslim, Turks, Christians 2. Kimis favorite magazine, <u>Photography Today,</u> has an article about cameras. 3. A. declarative B. interrogative C. exclamatory D. imperative 4.

Your name
Your street address
Your city, state   zip

                    Monti Banks
                    34 Drift Street
                    Day Creek, Oregon   97429

---

5. AMV/RA: Although the library doesn't open until ten, it offers a variety of activities including a noon-time story hour and an evening stress seminar at 7 P.M.

DAY 175: 1. Has, Mary, How, Eat, Fried, Worms, Horne, Public, Library 2. "Can't you make the <u>t's</u> on the sign larger?" asked Barry. 3. to look, to become, to remain, to feel, to seem, to appear, to taste, to sound, to stay, to smell, to grow, to be (is am, are, was, were, be, being, been) 4. Her (pronoun used as an adjective), funny, witty, that, hilarious 5. AMV/RA: Having received our letters concerning the freeway proposal, the governor responded likewise. The letters concerning the proposed freeway were sent to the governor who responded by mail.

DAY 176: 1. The, Orlando, Reading, Council, Mayor, Cortez, Patina, Hotel 2. Although everyone's choice was water-skiing, I'd rather go fishing. 3. A. parties B. ceilings C. elk (elks = second preference) D. patience 4. his (**Someone** is singular.) 5. AMV/RA: Taking a bath and putting on pajamas at seven o'clock, the little ones are read a book until their eight o'clock bedtime. In preparation for an eight o'clock bedtime, the little ones take a bath and put on pajamas; someone then reads a book to them.

DAY 177: 1. After, Bolshevik, Revolution, Communist, Party, Russia 2. Her idea, the one about self-inflating balloons, caught an inventor's attention. 3. mother 4. <u>bank</u> <u>is</u> 5.
AMV/RA: Dad repaired the chair once; its second breaking resulted in Dad throwing it away. When the chair which Dad repaired broke again, it was thrown away.

DAY 178: 1. In, Lancaster, County, Pennsylvania, Dutch, Amish 2. Susan, her voice soft, replied, "You're the ex-convict who's now our mission's leader." 3. <u>Cabot</u> and <u>group</u> ; <u>sailed</u> and <u>claimed</u> 4. I 5. AMV/RA: Of the two plants in the brass planter, the living ficus and the silk one, the former is shedding its leaves. The brass planter's living ficus is shedding its leaves; the silk one, of course, is not.

DAY 179: 1. Our, Spanish, Mexican, Cinco, Mayo 2. A. the play, <u>Ivan</u> B. the book, <u>Playful Poetry</u> C. the movie, <u>Conrad</u> D. the magazine, <u>Hair Ideas</u> 3. gone: <u>could have gone</u> 4.
AMV/RA: Jones Company / 567 East Belmont / Sedalia, CO 80315 5. AMV/RA: Having been involved in a recent accident, the two year old van had a cracked windshield and a dent in its back door. Although the van was only two years old, it had a cracked windshield and a dented back door due to a recent accident.

DAY 180: 1. Last, Trans, European, Tengri, Khan, Tien, Shan, Mountains, Asia 2. Morisa's dad, the self-reliant leader, is here; you'll want to meet him. 3. laid 4. A. fragment B. sentence C. run-on D. fragment E. fragment 5. AMV/RA: In making that dessert, add boiling water to the ingredients, add ice water next, stir until the mixture is dissolved, and then chill. The following steps are necessary to make this dessert: add boiling water to the package ingredients, add ice water, stir until dissolved, and then chill.